What's
Your
Sabotage?

The Last Word
in Overcoming Self-Sabotage

Alyce Cornyn-Selby

BEYNCH   PRESS

Other books by Alyce Cornyn-Selby:
    Procrastinator's Success Kit
    Take Your Hands Off My Attitude!
    Did She Leave Me Any Money?
    I Don't Have To & You Can't Make Me!
    I'm Going to Change My Name & Move Away!
    Making Your Mark: That's Marketing
    Alyce's Fat Chance
    Teamwork & Team Sabotage
    Why Winners Win

www.justalyce.com

Published by BEYNCH PRESS PUBLISHING COMPANY
1928 S. E. Ladd Avenue
Portland, OR 97214
503-232-0433

Contents

Chapter 1
What on Earth is going on here?

> **"We know when we're doing something**
> **that's not good for us because**
> **the voice that resides in the center of our heads**
> **can be a pretty vigilant nag.**
> **As long as we cling to habits**
> **that aren't life-enhancing,**
> **we only steal from our potential."**
> —Sarah Ban Breathnach
> in *Simple Abundance*

Welcome to the creative world of Self-sabotage—what I like to call: The Fascinating Art of Being Human. It's a world that would challenge Sherlock Holmes. If you love a mystery, welcome!

Guarantee: Television will be boring after this.

Self-sabotage is when we say we want something and then go about making sure it doesn't happen.

We are mysteries to ourselves! We have no idea why we say we want to lose 20 pounds *while we are eating a hot fudge sundae*. Or why we say we want to get the garage cleaned out and 52 weeks later it still isn't done.

Self-sabotage is baffling but it is infinitely fixable. It does not need to continue. After reading this book you'll have a *choice*.

To be without choice is a form of slavery, even if it is of our own making. That lack of freedom—to *not be able* to pick a weight and then weigh it, for instance—is high octane frustration.

"I can't keep my hands off the donuts."
"I can't keep my hands off the intern."
"I can't keep my hands on money."
"I can't keep myself organized."

"I can't keep a relationship."
"I can't keep this up much longer."

This is being backed into a corner—by your own behavior. It's saying: "I have this mess and I can't seem to stop doing this."

Self-sabotage is:
...New Year's resolutions shattered before February 1.
...promising yourself to get in shape, buying the exercise equipment and then watching it collect dust.
...renting a cabin in the woods to write your Great American Novel and returning home without a page written.
...being stuck in traffic at 11:45 pm April 15 with all the other people who have put off their taxes again this year.
...having a stack of late fees because of overdue books/parking tickets.
...promising yourself to take control of your finances and then never once seeing a zero due on your credit cards.
...signing up for a college course and then not showing up for class.
...calling an important meeting and "forgetting" to invite key players.
...discussing cholesterol and calories over Big Macs.
...getting into and out of relationships as if they were socks.
...having your moonlighting clients meet you at your regular job.
...being financially strapped and buying expensive jewelry or tools.
...getting your prescription filled and never taking the medicine.
...having a collection of printed stationery and never writing a letter.
...a closet full of unopened or once used appliances.
...promising yourself that "some" day you're going to learn line dancing, play a guitar/piano or sing.
...restarting a new food plan and whipping up a batch of cookie dough ostensibly for others, then having to make *another* batch of cookie dough because you ate the first one.

...paying for a membership and then doing nothing with it.

...a stack of self-help books, without a cracked spine in the bunch (never opened).

...foreign vacation tour books and pamphlets but no passport.

...leaving wet towels on the bathroom floor for your Felix Unger spouse.

...broken promises to children.

...letting insurance lapse.

It's not: "Are you sabotaging?" It's: "What are you sabotaging *today*?"

Some say, "This behavior is not logical!" And I say, "If logic prevailed, advertising would look like legal briefs."

Believe it or not, you're going to find a Very Good Reason (a higher need) for your mysterious behavior. It *will* make sense. When you discover it (called "cracking the code") you may be jolted but frequently you'll laugh. You may shake your head and say, "Wow, that's amazing." You'll have a sense of wonderment about yourself that is endearing. You'll find yourself admiring the efficient mechanisms that got you where you are—even if where you are is 100 pounds overweight like I was.

I developed a system for overcoming self-sabotage. Less sophisticated Model T versions have been around for 30 years. In your hands now, you have the super-charged, fuel efficient, tilt-air-cruise version—it will get you there faster and in comfort.

For more than 15 years I have taught this system to Air Force fighter pilots, bank presidents, nurses, janitors and even FBI agents. I go all over the United States, Great Britain and Canada speaking at conferences, conventions and management retreats. It takes a minimum of an hour and a half to teach the system. The University of Illinois School of Management called the program, "The only course that could change your life." (Thank you to everyone of the thousands who have watched me do the Self-Sabotage program and then told me about the tremendous things you've done with it.)

I have a small internal reaction when I read or when I hear, "This can change your life!" I think, hmmmmm, there are lots of things I *don't want* changed. I wonder if this is going to change those things? I think it's pretty audacious for someone to think or write or say that I should CHANGE MY LIFE. I don't really want to change my life; I want to tweak some of my goofy behavior. I just want to dial in on a goal and then do it. I want to decide what I want to do (more organized, get the garage cleaned, finish reading a book, finish writing a book, be true to a spouse, weed things, take accordion lessons, whatever) and then, without a lot of internal wailing or cajoling, just make it happen. I want to trust that I'll live up to my promises to myself. I just want to talk to myself and really mean it. I want to live a simple Nike sort of life and Just Do It! Of course, the result of this would be that it would change my life.

What makes someone on the brink of success suddenly push the self-destruct button? What makes you work to get the weight off and then just put it back on again? What makes you spend money you don't have? What makes YOU the biggest, toughest obstacle you have to deal with in Life? Why aren't you on your side? Why are you your own worst enemy?

"Know thyself."

Well, you didn't come with an instruction manual!

I don't know of any better way to "know thyself" than the method outlined in this book. You're going to be on a first name basis with yourself like you've never been before. You'll discover that there's been a lot of talking going on inside your head but nobody's been listening. Now you'll actually have the opportunity to *influence yourself*—to say you're going to do something and then do it.

I use this system to maintain a 100-pound weight loss, get my taxes done on time, finish writing assignments and run my business. I've used this system as a management tool—and turned a group of four departments from being downsized into one of the most award-winning communications teams in the United States.

It is not without humor. Frequently you'll have to laugh at what you discover. For you it may feel as if you've gone to the metroplex, bought your ticket, settled in to watch a movie and it's awful, then realizing you can take your ticket and move to another theatre and see a movie you really enjoy.

This book teaches you how to recognize a sabotage when you see it—not hind sight but *while you're in it.* You'll use easy-to-follow exercises, simple things that can get you unstuck, help you to become the organized, satisfied person you think you want to be. In just a few pages this book can help you transform only the parts of your life you *want* changed.

What **will** be required:
- creativity
- willingness to stretch the limits of conventional thought
- ability to listen
- attention
- alone time

What **may** be required:
- negotiation skills
- courage
- compassion (ability to cut yourself some slack)

What **will not** be required:
- self-esteem
- good attitude

Do you need self-esteem to get your taxes done on time?

Do you need self-esteem to eat a tomato instead of a donut?

Reported on *20/20*: convicts scored higher on self-esteem tests than college students. One Oregon psychologist said: "There's never been a study to link self-esteem with achievement."

"About 46% of college freshmen have to take at least one remedial class. Students who do well in high school are often poorly prepared for college assignments. Reason: To protect their self-esteem, students are being given unrealistic ideas about their abilities," says Clifford Adelman, senior research analyst, U.S. Department of Education.

When you think about it, does it really require self-esteem to clean your garage? organize your office? show up on time?

This book is not about self-esteem. It's about action. It's about getting you to do what you say you want. Life may be more pleasant if you have positive self esteem but you won't need it here.

How do people change? People change when they serve the real need of the voice within that's stopping them—when they understand that there is a higher need inside.

I don't think there's anything wrong with being fat. I do think there's something wrong with being *unhappy about* being fat, however. And a lot of people are unhappy with being fat.

If you're totally happy being fat, be fat!

This book is a tool for people who no longer want to be unhappy in their lives and want to achieve real results and realize their wants. If you're fat and you're happy being fat, then being thin is not one of your goals. I'm not here to give you a goal. I'm here to help you achieve the goals *you have for yourself.*

If you *think* like everybody else, you'll *be* like everybody else: limited, mystified, unable to solve self-sabotage, not in control and like 60% of Americans, unhappy about their weight. Keep thinking the same way you're thinking now and you'll get the same results you've always gotten.

"The greatest undeveloped territory in the world lies under your hat." We're going to use your head for something besides a hat rack. When we're finished, you will probably say: "I'd rather play with my mind than do just about anything."

Procrastination is—hands down—our #1, favorite form of self-sabotage.

If you want to get yourself to stop procrastinating, just write a book on procrastination. Nobody will let you get away with procrastinating after that! I know because I became the High Priestess of Procrastination (thanks for the title, Jerry) when I wrote *The Time Sabotage: The Last Word in Overcoming Procrastination* (formerly titled: *Procrastinator's Success Kit)*. It is still the best book on the subject of putting it off—that's the sabotage of your time. Procrastination is our favorite form of self-sabotage. But it's just *one* form.

Because I wrote the book on procrastination, people would come up to me and say, "Oh, procrastination! I am a master procrastinator!" and I would respond with this question: "Have you ever had your refrigerator break down and then put off calling the refrigerator repairman...for 3 months?" The response was always the same, "Oh, my, no—who would ever do *that?*" And I would say, "I know the person who did that. HE is a master procrastinator. The rest of us are just rank amateurs."

The system for wrestling with and getting past procrastination is also applicable to other sabotages—weight, finances, relationships, for instance. People use the system for all sorts of things. I did too. (I often wondered about people who would buy a book on procrastination and then immediately sit down and read it—if you're really a procrastinator, don't you have to let the book age on your nightstand a little bit first?)

People wanted to be told stories of how others had "cracked the code" of their sabotage, partly to self-discover comparable lives and partly because it's so interesting. To understand the baffling behavior of others is a marvelous thing! It makes the whole of Life less fuzzy, less stupid, more comprehensible.

Self-sabotage is like a grocery store of behavior and procrastination is only the produce department. There's a whole lot more out there and I wanted a book about the whole store.

I got fired up to write this book because of watching a) my best friend and b) the President of the United States both nearly self-destruct simultaneously before my eyes. Both scenarios were mind-numbingly frustrating. In both cases everyone was focused on the details of what the behavior actually was (and there was a lot of "How could he/she do that? Risk that?") instead of calling it what it was: self-sabotage. And without tending to the sabotage, both parties, of course, are doomed to repeat it.

My friend (who was sabotaging her time, her space, her finances and her career) sent me a marketing flyer about an upcoming seminar. The seminar's title was in bold headline letters: "Dealing Effectively With Unacceptable Employee Behavior" and my friend had written under that: "Hey, no problem. Now if only I could deal with my own unacceptable behavior!"

Newsweek, August 1998: "One evening, 22-year old Monica Lewinsky brought a pizza to him (President Bill Clinton). There, in the dying light of 1995, Bill Clinton managed to wreck his presidency; to ensure a second term and paralyze it; to save his legacy and soil it." The President of the United States proceeded to have "sex of a kind" with a White House intern and then, in subsequent months and years, evidently lied to family, friends, lawyers, investigative bodies, colleagues and the press about it. In another *Newsweek* article: "Clinton is fighting: to rescue his reputation from himself."

That's as accurate a description of self-sabotage as you can get.

The actual behavior itself didn't concern me nearly as much as the fact that it was *without question* self-sabotage …with both my friend and with the president.

The fact that the most powerful leader in the world was sabotaging his job rattled me far more than dress stains, phone sex and cigars. Those things are the trappings of the behavior. They're vivid and good fodder for the press but ultimately not enough to even warrant an official chastising. What is far more serious, however, is that the sabotage causing these fiascoes has gone, evidently "untreated." The underlying motivations are still there and still active.

I was quoted in *USA Today:*

"*Time* magazine says, 'Clinton beat the odds in 1992 when he promised to behave, and Americans believed him. He has known ever since that another sex scandal could finish him. Yet he risked his presidency on a reckless dalliance.'

"I have written and lectured extensively on the subject of self-sabotage for more than 15 years. Clinton is now the poster child for this behavioral phenomenon.

"Any philandering husband in the country could have done a better job of having an affair. With everything to lose, Clinton chose the worst possible partner for a tryst, left phone messages *knowing* they were bring taped, embraced her in public, gave and received gifts and met in the White House knowing that all visitors' names are recorded.

"Isn't it clear by now that we have a more serious problem here? He is sabotaging his presidency, his job.

"After promising he'd never do it again and living the most public life an American can live, he chose as his playmate a person who collects bodily fluids as souvenirs.

"This national horror is the classic case of self-sabotage. When you're nicknamed 'The Comeback Kid' then you have to keep creating things to come back from. It gives me an uneasy feeling to wake up knowing that my country is being led by a person engaged in sabotaging his career.

"We should be grateful that he has chosen sex as his method rather than something involving national security.

"I am concerned that unless Clinton discovers the source of his sabotage, he will continue it…and it may be worse than a sexual 'dalliance' next time. Career counselors help people like Clinton every day. His recklessness leaves us all vulnerable, and it is obvious he needs professional help."

I suddenly found myself on 70 radio stations across the country making sense to the Americans who heard it or read it. I suggested to the *New York Times* that a 10-point list called "Adultery 101" be posted in the White House for future presidents. This list is a simple guide that most married Americans just "know" about how to have an affair without involving the rest of the country. Common sense, as usual, is anything but common.

Leslie Stahl said it well in an interview in *Modern Maturity:* "This is such a Greek tragedy. So much promise. It's as if Clinton feels he doesn't deserve for things to go well and has to ruin it. Or the other interpretation: that he can't enjoy life unless there's danger involved."

It sort of makes procrastinating on your taxes pale by comparison, doesn't it? Sure, you've sabotaged your weight and you've rubbed the numbers off your credit cards a few times. But you're a motivated genius compared to some people.

When you want to ask "What the hell did he/she do *that* for?" reach for this book. You'll be able to answer that question for yourself.

"It's almost as if another part of the mind takes charge," one patient reported to a California psychiatrist.

You have a legitimate desire to end your self-sabotage and this book will show you how to do just that. But I hope this also gives you the perspective that self-sabotage, when left unchecked, causes enormous problems, not just for the people doing it but for everybody else. When it affects others, it is "behavioral pollution." It fouls everything. We pollute our personal economies with misuse of our money. We pollute our bodies with sugar and cigarettes thus saddling our spouses with having to live with us and our crippling diseases. We pollute the workplace when we sabotage a co-worker.

The system in this book is not controversial; you will "know" it when you hear it. It will resonate. If you experience any momentary resistance, it is because the sabotage is in danger of being altered. It has a Very Good Reason for wanting to stay with you.

Mike Tyson has done it. Cher has done it. Dennis Rodman has done it. Oprah's done it. Leona Helmsley's done it. The British Royal family has replaced polo and fox hunting with it. Heads of major corporations have done it. Your parents have done it. I've done it. You've done it. Self-sabotage. You're in good company. Good, but frustrated, company.

Human behavior will finally begin to make sense.

Prepare yourself for a Great Adventure. Become a "fresh traveler" open to sights and experiences, embracing both comfort and discomfort—sort of like a trip to Europe. But we're going into the darkest continent, the one between your ears. The last great frontier isn't outer space, it's inner space. There's comedy in there, surprising rationales, goofy wiring, mysteries that may remain mysteries and protection, protection, protection.

Pack a travel journal, pack binoculars, pack sunscreen, pack your sense of discovery, just don't forget to pack a sense of humor. Where we're going you won't need money; you'll need something even more rare and valuable: Quiet Time. Because your brain works so fast, it probably won't require *lots* of time. You'll discover that solitude is your ally, your secret weapon and a tool.

You can keep your sabotaging behavior as long as you want. It won't be wrenched from you as if you've had your passport confiscated. Your "baggage" will, unfortunately, not be lost. You'll start your journey thinking you're alone but after Chapter 3 you'll discover that you're really on a group tour. An excursion. A cruise. And you've brought all your best friends with you.

> **"The most foreign country is within.**
> **We are our own dark continent,**
> **we are our own savage frontier."**
> —Alice Walker

Well, it'll all make sense in a minute. You'll see. Welcome to the wonderful world of self-sabotage. Make sure your tray table is in its upright and locked position. Make sure your seat belt is strapped low and tight. In the unlikely event of a water landing, this book will become your flotation device.

Chapter 2
When is it NOT sabotage?

**"I'm making a list of all the things
I ought to do before I die.
It's my oughtobiography."**
—Internet humor

Human behavior did not make a lot of sense to me when I began my search for the Perfect Performance Appraisal. I was a manager for a company that had a typical system for evaluating employee performance. It was a flawed system. I didn't know what a good system would look like, since I'd never seen one but I knew that the one we had was not good. It demotivated people.

If you're going to create a performance review system that works, you'll need to research the question: "What motivates people to do good work?" That research should lead you to: "What motivates people to *work?*" There's an abundance of research on that one question but I can sum it up for you succinctly. The top seven reasons of why people work can be explained in these four words:

to have an effect.

People work in order to have an effect—on some thing or some body.

As a manager, my role changed when I comprehended the above statement. It meant that it was my job to make my staff aware that their behavior was having an effect on the whole picture of the company. Every action either added to or subtracted from our department's effort and the organization as a whole. I wanted that message immediate and vivid.

Nowhere is this more appropriate than in the performance review. These pages, called a Performance Appraisal, are supposed to represent an employee's efforts for an entire year. They usually end up reflecting the three weeks prior to the review and in most cases do not reflect a person's entire contribution.

When I received my first full year Performance Review from my boss, he had rated me highly, given me the maximum raise allowed and had properly filled out the company forms. And yet, I was so upset from the experience, I left for four days and went to Canada for a much needed "vacation."

You may ask: "What, are you crazy? What did you have to be upset about?"

During my drive to Canada, barely cognizant of the scenery going by—what I call "Windshield Time"—I pondered just those questions. It came down to a couple of things:

a) This document was not a reflection of one year's efforts and the most challenging year of my life up to that point. Ordinary things that I just did as a matter of course were highlighted. Things that had been brutal challenges, requiring all I had as a human, had not been mentioned at all.

b) I knew I wasn't a perfect employee. There's no such animal. Where was the coaching and direction I needed to improve and develop? Where was the direction for the next year's work? Where was the investment in me, as a manager, to get even better and qualified for more responsibility?

I remember hearing the Beatles singing something about sunshine on my car radio. The light began to dawn. I realized that my boss was not really at fault—he filled out the forms as instructed, as he'd always done for everyone. Then it occurred to me: there's nothing wrong with him; there's something wrong with the *system*. The system wasn't just the forms; they were a paper straitjacket.

1. The system was applied to production workers, secretarial, management, creative staff—one-size-fits-all kind of performance review that ended up not fitting anybody.

2. There was no opportunity on the form to cover any traits, habits or accomplishments other than what the form asked.

3. There was no available paper vehicle for the employee to comment on their own performance, ask for changes, request direction or education.

4. There was no area to give constructive coaching for the future.

I decided that no one on my staff should have to experience what I had experienced. If they cared about their jobs, as I most definitely did, they'd be let down and possibly insulted by such a system. It seemed that the only reasonable thing to do was: create our own system.

We did that. As a group. But only after I found a library of information about other performance review systems. I started collecting them like stamps. I got them from the military, utility companies, high tech companies, banks, manufacturing and government. I learned from a Harvard study to the American Management Association that **97% of American employees do not like their performance review systems.** I also learned that the number one reason people leave their employment is directly or indirectly related to the performance review system. This makes having a lousy performance review system a *very expensive luxury.*

I collected so much data that I needed the perspective of other people to simplify all the information. I also needed to know what the people I would be evaluating thought. It only took three well-organized staff meetings to create the questions that we all wanted to see on a performance review form. It seems that everybody has an opinion on this subject and my group was blessedly verbal. Everyone had input and we didn't stop until everybody was happy with the new forms.

We also decided that the most important person in the process was the *person being evaluated* and that this person should have first shot at looking at their contribution on paper. We created a set of blue forms that allowed the employee to comment on their growth, their accomplishments and even make requests for changes in their work environment. I decreed that no supervisor or manager should begin the performance review process without having the employee fill out their own forms first. Who better?

I also thought that employees should keep track of their own behavior. I coined the phrase "self-validating" employees. Otherwise a manager can feel as if management is a kind of adult day-care, that all these people are like kids in a playpen and every day is just one personnel problem after another. When a manager feels that way, a) life is a drag and b) you can bet there's an ineffective performance review system in place. The most important thing to remember is c) it's fixable.

A system is supposed to:
Save
Your
Sanity
Time
Energy and
Money

I managed four departments and we all started using our new system. Because the forms were "sent up the line" and also into Personnel, they were noticed. In pretty short order, my division chief saw the value of our new system and adopted it for all the other departments. Within two years, the entire company had embraced our system.

I didn't set out to change the company's system; I just wanted something that worked for my department. Since I had both creative staff and production staff, we also knew that if it could fit us, chances were, it would work for most other job functions too.

In the process of doing all this and having a happy outcome, I followed this research trail of questions:
- What motivates people to do good work?
- What motivates people to work?
- What motivates people to do *anything?*
  and this led me to:
- Why are people sabotaging their own efforts?

Had my boss been sabotaging me or the system? Or did we have a system that wasn't working? This is an extremely important question to ask.

Managers procrastinate on doing performance reviews because deep inside they know their flawed systems don't motivate. (A system problem.)

Dog trainers look at this question when faced with "problem behavior" dogs. Too many highly trained dogs have been featured heroes on television with the stories of how they were just hours from being "put down" because of their unruly behavior. In the hands of a different person, they changed into miracle-performing dogs.

Psychologists look at this question when kids are "unmanageable." If a child throws tantrums at home but acts fine at Grandpa's house, chances are this isn't a chemical problem, it's a system problem. System problems are environments that inadvertently encourage unwanted behavior.

In personal/intimate relationships: is there a system in place between these two people to deal with conflict? It's not the *subject* of the disagreement (finances, sex, how to raise the children) that's important—it's how do they handle the issues they face? Is there courage and communication and negotiation? Or is there procrastination, boiling points, accusations and ultimatums? Is this a people problem or a system problem?

When you see unwanted behavior, ask: Is this a system problem or a people problem? If you're constantly complaining about your clients, then you've created a system for doing business that isn't working. Change your system and the client behavior will change.

System problems are usually easier to spot in work situations. Are mistakes (in manufacturing or communication) being made because there aren't enough approval checks along the way? (A system problem.) Or do we have enough checks and an employee isn't using the system? (A people problem.)

I've seen too many "problem employees" in corporate life who were transferred to other departments and then became stars.

The reworking of our performance review system taught me to recognize the difference between a system problem and people problems.

Once we had a very positive performance review system in place, what would be the result? All the good things you can expect like improved morale, improved communication and higher productivity happened. So what would be the excuse of an employee *not* performing within this positive environment? Ah, the plot thickens!

Enter: self-sabotage!

If you've decided that your systems have been reworked, polished, oiled and they're working perfectly for you and yet unwanted behavior is still there, it's time to examine the possibility that someone is sabotaging.

When I was given those four departments to manage, they were scheduled for down-sizing. Within seven years we had become the most award-winning communications team of its kind in the country. From the outside, that looks remarkable. From the inside, it felt like a logical progression concentrating on a people-friendly system that worked.

How can you tell if it's a System Problem or a People Problem?

System Problem	People Problem
There's more than one person doing this behavior.	The behavior is clearly "against the rules"—stealing, lying, fraud.
There's no consensus about anything—nobody seems to be "on the same page"	The person clearly knows the rules and "knows better."
It keeps happening over and over again but with different people.	The repeat offender is always the same person.
You have a well-used Plan B	A promise broken.
They don't do this behavior in a different context or environment.	It appears irrational.
Nothing is clearly defined.	You've given direction clearly more than once.

Chapter 3
The Course—Part I

**"If you want to get closer to personal
and professional excellence,
this material will take you there."**
Daily Journal of Commerce

People are never more creative than when they're sabotaging their own efforts...and frequently never more productive than when they're procrastinating.

What did she say? Am I reading that right?

Yep. A deputy executive director for the Port of Portland observed: "Oh, yes, I understand this one. My house was never in better repair than when I was working on my Ph.D.!"

Bea Borden, vice-president of marketing for a large real estate resort, says, "I'm never more productive than when I have something on my to-do list that I don't want to do!"

Everybody has their own personal little thing that they like to sabotage (for me it's tax preparation). We may not recognize our own behavior but people who live with us and people who work with us—they've got our number.

Case in point: I'm not what you call a real domestic person. The most domestic thing about Alyce is, she was born in this country. My idea of cleaning a house is to buy lower watt light bulbs. And on my tombstone, it will not read: her family liked the food.

One Saturday afternoon in the spring I was in the kitchen polishing the silver. My daughter came around the corner, took one look and said, "Oh, tax time?"

See, that's how it works. We are *least* likely to recognize our own sabotaging behavior. So let's look at other people's behavior...it's safer and easier.

List of Possible Sabotaging Behaviors
- "accidents"
- procrastination
- losing weight and gaining weight and losing weight and gaining weight and...
- a string of relationships
- a string of jobs
- something that appears on you "to do" list more than 10 times
- hearing yourself make commitments, then watching yourself not keep them
- lateness
- "forgetfulness"

List of Common Things that Get Sabotaged
- weight loss ("I must be big-boned." or "It's in my genes.")
- exercise ("Who says I need to exercise? My body has outlasted four cars!")
- credit cards ("Rub the numbers right off that card!")
- cleaning out the garage...attic...closet...or back of your car
- writing thank you notes
- taxes and financial planning in general
- wills, organ donor directives, estate planning
- things that really matter: dream destination trips, education goals, "tough love" communication, "Some-Day-I'm-Gonna" List

I researched and wrote the book *Why Winners Win* and in that book I identified six things winners have and three things they don't seem to have. The older I get the more I can simplify it: **Winning is the absence of sabotage.**

I also wrote *Teamwork and Team Sabotage* and I can see that **teamwork is the absence of sabotage.** When no one is sabotaging the effort, we call them a team.

Few things in life are as colorful, dynamic and interesting as self-sabotage.

I learned:

You cannot sell a product or service until you first deal with self-sabotage.

You cannot lose the weight and keep it off until you deal with self-sabotage.

You cannot write the book until you deal with self-sabotage.

You cannot get to where you say you want to go until you deal with self-sabotage.

You cannot *succeed* without dealing with self-sabotage.

Why would someone say they wanted something and then go about doing just the opposite? Why are we on "self-destruct"?

News alert: Somebody tried to sabotage the Office of the President! Unfortunately, it was Bill Clinton.

Somebody's trying to sabotage your Life! Unfortunately, it's the person who is supposed to be your best friend. It's *you*.

The dictionary defines "sabotage" as: a) deliberate subversion, b) an act tending to hamper or hurt.

Health Alert!: Recent research reported that 80% of us do not follow through on our doctor's prescriptions! Some of us never get the prescription filled. Some of us get the prescription filled, then don't take *any* of the pills. Some of us get the pills, take a few and "forget" to take the rest. Few of us, only 20% it turns out, actually follow the doctor's direction.

And yet…you want your medical person to have graduated the top in their class and to stay current on all medical information. You expect them to use every ounce of their diagnostic brain power to aid you. If you don't hold up your end (take the pills, quit smoking), then you might just as well see the doc who graduated last in his/her class. Their efforts should mirror yours, right? Not going to floss? Then go looking for a cut rate dentist. It must be enormously frustrating for doctors to meet patients enthusiastically when 80% of us are going to go on sabotaging our health *anyway*. This has everything in the world to do with TEAMWORK. Any survivor of cancer will tell you that their success was a team effort. Are you on your own medical team? Are you on your own side?

Becoming an Expert in Self-Sabotage

By the end of the next segment you will be an expert in the area of self-sabotage. The lights will go on for you. I have presented these illustrations to thousands of people for over ten years and related two of them in a book called the *Procrastinator's Success Kit* (retitled: *The Time Sabotage*). Nothing seems to be more effective in conveying the mystery of self-sabotage than these two stories.

The Miracle of the Brown Volvo

Imagine that you own a brown Volvo. You drive your brown Volvo to the grocery store and you don't get it in the angle parking just right and pretty soon the car begins to look like it's been "tapped on all four corners." You take your brown Volvo through the car wash and you neglect to lower the antennae and that gets broken off. You forget the 3,000 mile check and then the 5,000 mile check. You don't remember to have the oil changed. A friend of yours with a history of drinking problems, steps up to you and wants to borrow your brown Volvo to drive to the airport and you immediately hand over the keys.

Each of these events *individually* doesn't mean much.

Then one day you're on your way to your brown Volvo with a friend or, better yet, a business associate who looks at the car and says to you, "Gee, when are you going to get rid of your old Volvo?" (It's not that old.)

That does it! You take the brown Volvo and you trade it in on that cute little red sports car you've been passing every day on your way to work in the morning. You get into the red sports car and you say to yourself, "Ah, this is better! This is more like me!"

What's been going on here?

A sabotage of the brown Volvo, perhaps? It is interesting to note that your sabotaging behavior *began* the day the red sports car appeared in the showroom window.

At no time, however, were you *aware* of your sabotage. You won't recognize your own sabotage for this reason: in between those incidents with the brown Volvo, there were several thousand other incidents in your life. Until the mishaps and memory lapses are stacked up together in one paragraph, you can't see what's really going on with the brown Volvo. Most of the facts were so insignificant that they weren't worth remembering. They were, however, signposts of behavior.

For many people it's not OK to buy a car and then just turn around and buy a different car. We have to have a Very Good Reason for trading and lacking that, we have to trash what we have in order to justify trading it in on something new. **Recognize that people are doing this with *relationships* and with *jobs*.** We can't just trade in the old one for a new one without *trashing the old one first.*

Why not?

Because if we do, somebody will ask: "What's *wrong* with the old one?" What's wrong with the old car? What's wrong with the old job? What's wrong with the old spouse? And we don't want to be wrong.

Time for the Big Ah-Ha

We want to be "right." In fact, we will work harder to hear the words "You're right" than to hear the words "I love you." This is a significant factor in understanding human behavior. And if you wonder about its power, try this on for size...

Let's say you're a lousy housekeeper. Your friends know you're a lousy housekeeper, the family knows you're a lousy housekeeper, the neighbors know you're a lousy housekeeper—what do you have to do to be "right"?*

You have to be a lousy housekeeper, don't you?

So what happens if you start cleaning up the place? Someone will say to you, "What's *wrong?* Is Grandma coming?"

* From Wally Minto's Alpha Awareness course

Let's say you're a lousy poker player. Your family knows you're a lousy poker player, your buddies know you're a lousy poker player, your co-workers know you're a lousy poker player. What do you have to do to be "right"? You have to be a lousy poker player! What happens if you suddenly start winning? What will they say? "There's something *wrong*. You must be cheating!"

So in order to be "right" you have to continue being the same You that you've always been because everybody (including you) perceives that this is the Right You. This is why it can be so difficult to change from the person you are into the person you want to be. ***Any change is an admission that the old way was "wrong."*** And we can't stand that!

To be "right" all the time requires stagnation. ***The greatest deterrent to teamwork is people who want to "be right."*** They bog down meetings and stifle creativity. They can turn an innovative company into a home for zombies. "We tried that last year." Business is in such a constant state of flux that something that didn't work only six months ago, might work now.

The desire to be perceived as "right" is a major handicap. The reason people seem to function so well during a disaster is because they give up the right-wrong concept and go with what will work. Protocol and rules go out the window with the tornado and floods, replaced with anything that will give us what we need *now!*

MiniQuiz

Let's see how firmly entrenched you might be in this right-wrong trap. Below is a situation and there's an imperfect "right" solution, but there is also a perfect solution. See if you can guess it before you read it.

I want you want to purchase a vehicle and this is the *only* criteria:
- able to haul couch-sized items
- good suspension system
- covered haul-area for protecting items

- easy access to the haul-area
- used: low mileage
  perfectly cared for
  always garaged
  pampered, not driven harshly
  well maintained
  immaculate
- very inexpensive
- comfortable ride
- air-conditioned
  Your solution to this problem: _____.

If you suggested pickup truck, you'll have to buy a cover for it. That's a "right" answer. If you suggested van (mini or otherwise), your "right" answer may get shot down with trying to get "low mileage" and "very inexpensive" in one vehicle. If you suggested bus, you'll have to remove the seats and you may have to forego the immaculate part. If you suggested covered wagon for your "right" answer, we'll miss the air-conditioning.

What could possibly fit this wretched list? Give up what's "right" to drive for you and you'll have the solution.

How about a secondhand ambulance or better yet—a hearse? That fits the criteria perfectly. But it's probably not your "right" answer, is it?

"How it's going to look to your neighbors" was not part of the criteria. "Inconspicuous" was also not part of the criteria. "Easy to park" was not on the list. "Good gas mileage" was not on the list. Did you automatically add these things to your list and in so doing, eliminated the more perfect answer?

How does your mind accept the solution of a hearse?

You have internal criteria for all sorts of problems—you'd like solutions to all of them—but you a) don't list the criteria b) don't have *everything* listed on your criteria c) will only accept a "right" answer. As a result, you get standard solutions that will fit only part of your criteria and not the entire list. If people and things and situations always seem to be falling short in your life, you've probably got a death grip on being "right."

At least be willing to *think* differently and come up with

the perfect solution—like buying a hearse—even if you don't actually *do* the solution.

How many times have you felt that the "right" solution was "sticking it out" when you knew that the perfect solution was to leave? Was it while you were watching an overrated movie with a friend? Or something more serious like staying with a company that didn't value you?

I worked with a CEO who asked, "How can I get my employees to act the way they did the day the roof nearly blew off the building?" (The building is one of the largest warehouses in the United States and visible in satellite photographs.) When hurricane-sized winds began pulling the roof off, employees worked together efficiently to save product and each other. Unfortunately this team effort disappeared when the winds died down. When the disaster was over, the *esprit de corp* was over too.

When America was hammered with both a Great Depression and the Dustbowl, people had to drop what was "right" and did what was necessary. Those who survived it talk wistfully about these "good old days."

Can you think of a time in your life when you gave up the right-wrong concept? and did what worked instead?

When the Nimitz Freeway collapsed during the San Francisco earthquake in 1989, a woman was trapped in her car. Using all their efforts, the rescue squad was unable to free her. As the massive concrete settled on her, a surgeon was summoned to sever her leg so that she could be lifted to safety. She readily agreed to this, her space shrinking by inches every minute. The surgeon's saw was running when a fireman had one last idea. He inserted the Jaws of Life tool and used it *backwards*. When they pulled on the woman she slipped out like a fresh tuna.

"Right" thinking had almost cost her her life and nearly her foot.

There's a mania lose in the land now that says your home must have a Living Room. It may take up as much as 30% of your floor space. And yet, if you entertain a lot, you may use it only 8% of the time and then complain that you have no room in your house to set up your hobby. Or worse, you rent storage space for your excess stuff miles from your home. You have a choice piece of real estate—your living room—and as one woman told me, "It's the space I walk through every day to see if anyone has stolen the furniture." But having a Living Room is the "right" answer. Keeping the fly tying or sewing or photography darkrooms in a cold damp basement is a "right" answer.

Your "right" answers are standing between you and successful solutions.

We gravitate toward the familiar because we're driven and at the same time protected by an ego which only wants to be *right*.

So trade in that brown Volvo for the red sports car—or better yet, a hearse—put your canoe or your art project in your living room, be a stunning housekeeper if you want to or start winning at poker.

The Good Employee Who Wasn't

Here's the scene: I was a manager in Portland, Oregon and I had a position open in my department. We advertised and read resumes and interviewed people but we could not find anyone with the specialized skill to fill the position. So we advertised the position in Seattle and found a fellow I'll call Jim.

We liked his work and offered him the position. Jim accepted and we moved him, his wife and two kids to Oregon. Everything went along just great for about two years.

Then Jim began to take issue with minor things. Soon he wasn't getting along with people who brought him work. Next thing you know he wasn't getting along with other people on the staff. Like good modern-day managers we asked ourselves, "What have we done wrong that Jim is no longer enjoying his work with us?"

Jim's supervisor was having no luck with Jim's black moods. As things got worse, Jim's supervisor, a sensitive and effective manager, began to take Jim's behavior personally. We just kept expecting Jim to return to the Jim we had hired.

We went around on the horns of that dilemma for about two months when my boss finally said, "It looks like he's trying to get fired."

That had never occurred to me! It wasn't part of the framework of how I saw life. I had never heard of anything like that before! But, you know, it's hard to **see the picture when you're part of the frame.**

I started looking at Jim's behavior differently and after a very short amount of time I had to agree with my boss. When Jim had a moonlighting client deliver work to him at our company, there was no more pretending we didn't have a problem.

We gave Jim two choices: either go to out-placement counseling which essentially gets the employee out of the company, or go to a career counselor. (There are times during a manager's career when outside help is needed. Managers think they have to solve all employee problems when an outside professional could do a more efficient job. Handling an alcoholic employee, for example, needs an experienced hand.) Jim chose to see the career counselor.

After three sessions with the career counselor, Jim started coming to work with a smile on his face. I could hardly believe it. After months of progressive growling, Jim seemed completely turned around. I was guessing that the counselor had performed brain surgery on Jim because nothing had changed in the work environment. Jim's supervisor was relieved. I was elated. Harmony was restored. What had happened?

What Jim had managed to figure out—*with the help of the career counselor*—was what he *really* wanted was to move back to Seattle. It didn't have anything to do with the work, other staff members, his supervisor or me. He was homesick! Jim had a higher need to be in Seattle than to work for us. He just didn't know it. Not knowing your "higher need" is the major wrinkle in the self-sabotage phenomena.

The most important thing to remember about this story is: Jim could have passed a lie detector test saying that he wanted to work for us. He was totally unaware that there was a part of him that was so homesick that it was willing to get him fired to get back home. Remember: Jim is not an evil person and was not sent to Planet Earth just to annoy me, although it felt like that at the time. If he didn't understand his own behavior, he couldn't relate it to us. It took a competent career counselor to uncover it in just three sessions.

So why didn't Jim just realize he was homesick on his own and move back to Seattle? Remember I said he had a wife and two kids? If he had come home and said to his wife "I just quit my job" she would have killed him. But if he comes home and says "I just got fired," it would be "oh, poor Jim, it's okay! We'll move back to Seattle and start again. Everything will be fine."

Jim wasn't dishonest. He was no more aware of his inner drives than you may be of a slight and uncomfortable pressure somewhere in your body right now. Most of what is going on in our lives, isn't occurring to us.

The "right" solution in situations like this is: fire the employee. You probably thought of that already. The sabotaging employee puts a manager in a situation with few options left. However, firing someone is an enormously stressful task. It is more than *twice as stressful to do the firing as to be fired!* Having to fire an employee doubled a patient's risk for a heart attack.

Instead of the usual stressful "solution," we did what I call "living life gracefully" and that is, we helped Jim find a job in Seattle. We had a going-away party for him, he moved and sent us postcards. We all got to live happily ever after. And we came so close to having the typical ending to the story—the standard "right" answer of firing the employee.

I learned so much from Jim that I should have paid him for the experience. I learned to what lengths a good employee will go to get what they don't even know they want! I learned that we pay attention to the words and forgive the actions when it should be just the opposite. And I also learned that helping people get what they want, what they really, *really* want is good for all parties involved and I selfishly include myself in that. When you help people get what they want, you inadvertently help yourself. And I don't just mean the warm fuzzies you get from helping another human being. I mean, there are real benefits to you in terms of effectiveness and efficiency.

Courses in stress management will show you how to

deal with your stress. I'd like to cut the stress off at the pass before it even gets to me! The study of self-sabotage does that. ***Understanding self-sabotage can be the greatest stress reducer since meditation and Valium combined!*** With Jim, we discovered that stress can be avoided by a) realizing the problem isn't going away b) getting help c) comprehending the power of self-sabotage d) helping everybody get what they want.

> **"In my life's chain of events**
> **nothing was accidental.**
> **Everything happened according**
> **to an inner need."**
> —Hannah Senesh

Are you beginning to see how beautifully self-sabotage works?

There are two reasons I want to study self-sabotage:
1. I want to know if I'm doing it so that I can give myself the benefit of it—then I don't have to sabotage to get it.
2. I want to know if you're doing it so I can get out of the way! I want to be able to recognize self-sabotage in others because I don't like being an innocent bystander to somebody else's sabotage.

And, chances are, neither do you.

If you could have both of those things, it would be a great stress reducer, wouldn't it? You betcha!

So how do you recognize self-sabotage?

Fortunately it's pretty simple: ***there's a disparity between the words and the actions.*** The words are "I want to work for you" but the actions tell you something different. The words are "I want to live with you" but the actions tell you something different.

Now you're ready for:

Exercise 1

You may be tempted to just read the exercise and not do it. Instead, do it. When you see a blank line in this book, fill it. If you think you're going to want to hand this book off to someone else when you've finished it, buy them a copy so your own notes remain confidential. Don't short change yourself on these exercises. You've come too far to schlock it up now.

Think of somebody who is sabotaging something. Do not pick yourself. Yet. Select someone who is sabotaging their weight, their finances, their education, their careers...any sabotage that comes to mind. Do *not* write their name down. Just write a two to four word description of the sabotage:

_____

Now list two possible benefits that this person gets for this behavior.

Huh? If you're having trouble thinking of a benefit, this will help you get started: if nothing else, they may be getting attention for this behavior. Because you thought of them means that they are occupying a space in your awareness. Along with Coca Cola, *Star Wars* and BMW, this person has a *position* in your mind. You have given attention to it otherwise you wouldn't have thought of them. So "getting attention" is a common answer as a possible benefit. If you think your person is getting attention for this sabotaging behavior, write that down and then come up with one more benefit.

Hunches are acceptable here. You don't have to *know it for a fact*. That isn't necessary. For our purposes, guesses count.

Two Possible Benefits:
  1. _____
  2. _____

Don't read further until you've filled in those two blank lines. Two possible benefits. You have 90 seconds to fill in the two blanks above.

When I ask, "How many people picked 'gets attention' as one of the benefits of this sabotage?" usually between 60% and 70% of the participants raise their hands. There are two other benefits that show up most frequently. They are:

"The person that you picked...do they somehow *get off the hook* for some sort of responsibility by using this behavior?"

and

"Does this person somehow get to *control* a situation with this behavior?"

These three items (attention, responsibility and control) usually represent 90% of sabotage benefits. The huge shift in thinking you should be having right now is this: ***there's a benefit to sabotage.*** Somebody is getting something for it. And when you take 90 seconds to think about it from this perspective, you can see that it doesn't take being psychic or a Ph.D. to see what's going on. What is required, however, is that the question gets asked: what's the benefit? This changes everything.

90% Home Free test

Have you ever said: "There's somebody on the inside of me who..."? Or have you ever said: "Well, part of me wants to but part of me doesn't..."?

Have you ever wanted to buy something, told yourself you couldn't afford it, walked away from it and then had it "call" to you? Perhaps it was hours, perhaps it was days, but the thing called to you. So you went back to get it and on the way you heard two distinctly different voices in your head: "This is great! I can't wait to get my hands on it!" AND "This is the dumbest thing I've ever done—I can't afford this!"

If you've ever had this experience then you're 90% home free on solving any of your own self-sabotage.

Exercise 2

Have you made a recent purchase of a sizable nature—a house, a boat, a car, something that you had to part with large number dollars for? Were you recently tempted by an expensive appliance, sports equipment or jewelry?

✗ yes ____ no

When you found this item, did you just instantly buy it...or was there a conversation that took place in your head?

____ yes, there was a conversation

____ no, just bought it when I saw it ⟩ *Both!*

If you recognized that there was a conversation in your mind, then you are among the 95% of people who can recognize it. If you answered that you instantly bought this item, then you have had plenty of conversations with yourself about this in the past or you've got plenty of space *and* money.

Right this minute part of you wants to be doing something other than reading. How do I know that?

Because on the back end of many cars I read things that say, "I'd rather be sailing..." "I'd rather be shopping at Nordstrom's..." "I'd rather be bowling..."

Doesn't matter what we're doing—part of us still wants to be doing something else. Some people watch television with their thumbs firmly stuck on the channel button. They don't really want to see what's on television, they want to see what *else* is on television!

OK, so part of you wants to be doing something else. But part of you wants to know about self-sabotage so strongly and this is all sounding very accurate to you that you continue to read.

Exercise 3

Now I want you to come along with me and get inside the mind of someone who has just found a beautiful classic car. It's for sale. If we could get inside this person's head, we might hear a conversation that goes something like this:

"Look at this wonderful car!"

"Oooooo, it's expensive."

"Oh, but I would look so *good* pulling up at the ski lodge driving this car. I can just picture parking it at Timberline Lodge…"

"You buy this car, you won't have money to get on the slopes."

"Hmmmmmm. It's white. Probably hard to keep it looking clean."

"Oh, but look! It's got leather seats, polished wood dashboard."

"It gets high marks from *Consumer Reports*. I'll have this car a long time!"

"Look at the safety features on this car! I'd be really safe in this car."

"Yeah, well what are my relatives going to think when I pull up at the family reunion driving this car? I mean, this car is like over-the-top! My brother-in-law is probably going to ask for that $50 back that I borrowed from him…"

"Gee, it looks like it's doing 90 m.p.h. while it's parked! I wonder what the cops do when they see a car like this. I'll bet it gets a lot of tickets!"

"Hurry up and make a decision."

In the span of a few seconds, an internal meeting was held and at least six parts or characters attended. They brought their own agendas to the meeting and argued their cases. The car was bought or the car was left depending on the outcome of this meeting.

Chances are you have similar parts or voices on the inside of your head. These characters are running your life.

"I am large. I contain multitudes."
—Walt Whitman

Let's take another look at the conversation and this time we are going to put JOB TITLES on these various parts that will help identify them by their agendas, by their function inside your head.

As we do this I want you to imagine that you are the Chief Executive Officer of your own company. The different parts are different vice-presidents that report to you on various aspects of your life.

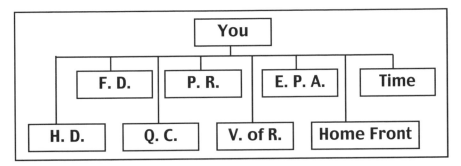

The first part who said, **"Isn't this a wonderful car?"** and **"I would look so good being seen with this car..."** **That's your internal PR Director.** Public relations. This is the person on the inside of you that is responsible for how your image is portrayed to others. This person dressed you this morning. The purpose of your internal PR director is to keep you looking "hip, slick and cool" all the time. Your internal PR Director is the one who is mortified when your co-worker tells you that you've had a piece of spinach between your teeth all afternoon. If you're the only one who shows up at the Halloween party wearing a costume—wow, the PR director screwed up BIG TIME. Your PR Director is the one who says, "They sent us a Christmas card last year, we'd better send them one this year."

This is a very important person inside of you. You wouldn't be where you are today if it weren't for your internal PR Director. Nobody wears a ballerina tutu to the grocery store— that's too bad, it would make it a different experience. It's not illegal to do such a thing. It's just that your internal PR Director simply won't allow it. You could make your life pretty uncomfortable for yourself without a competent PR director.

Some business people say it was easier *before* Casual Day was instituted in their offices. They knew exactly what to wear. The last thing they needed in that high stress, pre-coffee, rush hour time of the morning was choices about what to wear. For someone used to two choices (business suit or sweat suit) it's been agony to come up with a third wardrobe. The internal PR Director is confused and doesn't like confusion.

The next voice who says, **"It's expensive"** and **"If you get this car, you won't have enough money to get on the slopes"—this is your internal Financial Director** speaking to you. For some people, their internal Financial Directors are pit bulls. If you are one of these people, you can't get up and walk across the room unless your internal Financial Director says it's OK. But you also know people whose internal Financial Directors are either asleep, on drugs or aren't in there at all! They've never balanced their checkbooks in their lives, Visa card is always over the limit, they can go bankrupt three times in a lifetime and you know, it really doesn't bother them that much.

If we were to shake you upside down, however, you may be able to tell us how many coins are in your pockets before they hit the ground. Your internal Financial Director may issue bizarre advice like: go to Costco and buy peanut butter in a drum because it's only 17 cents a pound and you'll never get a price like that again.

It appears to be illegal in this country for people with matching internal Financial Directors to ever *marry.* Just doesn't seem to happen that often.

If you've ever pinched pennies for months and then blown your savings on an expensive luxury, then you have experienced an internal *power play,* not dissimilar to those that go on in corporations every week.

Then there's the part that says, **"It's white. Hard to keep clean. But durable. Will last a long time." This is your internal Voice of Reason,** that practical sense that advises and advises and advises until you wish they'd just put a sock in it. Some of what they have to say is verbatim from your mom's mouth and your dad's mouth. This is the internal character who must muscle their way past the PR Director and ask, "What kind of gas mileage does it get?" The agenda for the Voice of Reason is Let's-Be-Practical. Your internal Voice of Reason is probably the one inside you that's always trying to find a shorter route to the airport. Your Voice of Reason bought that brown Volvo. It keeps companies like L.L. Bean and Pendleton in business.

Then there's the part that says, **"Look at the safety features on this car! I'm going to be safe driving this car." This is your internal Health Director** speaking. This person is responsible for the bio-container that you're walking around in. Your body. This character will tell you to lose a few pounds, take your vitamins, floss and buckle up. And don't stand too near the edge. Their agenda is your physical safety. For the tenth time this year you may have read about the warning signs of cancer. Or you might have a soft spoken Health Director and not even *know* a dentist. "Don't run with scissors. Don't stand on that flimsy chair to change the light bulb. Unplug the toaster before you stick a knife in it." All of our internal Health Directors have varying degrees of power when it comes to affecting behavior.

There is a powerful part inside most people who says, **"What will the family think of this car?" This is your internal Home Front Director.** This person knows your position in the family unit. Even if you're estranged from your family, this voice exerts an influence. Similar to the PR Director, this voice follows directives from your specific family values in addition to mass media values.

It also understands your position in the family—golden boy, kissing cousin, family clown, black sheep, n'er-do-well, daddy's girl—and keeps you there with its advice. How comfortable would you be arriving at your next family gathering driving a white Rolls Royce? If you say, "not comfortable at all" then we can safely assume that your internal Home Front Director recognizes that you were never intended to earn more money than your parents. This director may say things like, "Don't get above your raisin'" or "Who do you think you are?"

Or you may have a Home Front Director that sounds like Franklin D. Roosevelt's mother who was not at all surprised when her son was elected President of the United States. Perhaps your family expects you to do well and you just do well. You're lucky.

Psychology spends most of its time unraveling these messages from the Home Front Director and how they are affecting your present behavior. A real family member does not have to be present, you know, for you to be influenced by their early messages. Many successful comedians got their stand up routines honed by trying to make their fathers laugh.

The last part says, **"Hurry up and make a decision" and this character is your internal Time Keeper.** Everyone has an internal clock and a voice that either watches that clock or ignores the clock. For some people, when you say the meeting starts at 8 o'clock, you do *not* mean 8:03. For other people, the meeting starts at 8 o'clock, you think you're doing well to stroll in at 8:15. Sense of time can be a cultural thing. One can reasonably expect a bus in Switzerland to run closer to schedule than a bus in Hawaii. (I have a pet theory that says it is the influence of palm trees that causes this—I think palm trees emit some sort of rays that cause people to abandon their internal clocks. Just a theory at this point.)

You may have an internal Time Keeper who will cause you to leave your fingerprints embedded in the steering wheel of your car when you're already 10 minutes late for an appointment and now there's a train guard going down over the road! People who seem to love time and are motivated by deadlines frequently chose jobs (media, for instance) that keep their internal Time Keepers active and interested.

So here are six internal directors that are commonly found inside the minds of most people. There are two others I'd like to introduce you to—you may recognize them too.

Say "howdy" to your internal **Environmental Protection Agency (EPA)** or what some people call their internal **Clean Freaks.** For some of you it's a cardinal offense to leave a dirty dish in a sink overnight. For some of you it's not time to clean until the dust bunnies are big enough to have names. Which is it for you?

A vacuum cleaner company instructs its sales people that you cannot sell a vacuum sweeper to anyone until you first determine their DTL—dirt tolerance level. That's it and you've got one.

Felix Unger and Oscar Madison (the Odd Couple) is what we have here. We all have a different idea about what "clean" is—we bring our sterling ideas into offices and work places every day. And our internal EPA's are at war with other people's EPA's. This War Front gets even more exciting in personal relationships. This seems to be the other area where people with matching EPA's rarely *marry*.

Legend has it that Lucille Ball would clean the little restrooms on airplanes—*had* to leave the space spic and span—because she didn't want anyone to think she was untidy.

You might be the kind of person who can't get started on a project until the top of your desk is clean. Or you may be someone who is actually *uncomfortable* in a too neat, too perfect, pillows-fluffed-and-arranged kind of world. I personally admire the person who posted a wooden sign in their weed patch that reads: Martha Stewart's Other Garden.

The last character or part I'm going to introduce you to is the **Quality Control (QC) Director.** This is the part who arrives at the work place with experience, education and maybe even devotion and leaves feeling like they've been wearing a sandpaper suit all day. Because of their experience and education, they have learned how things need to be done. They didn't fall off the turnip truck yesterday. They *know*. But because of that awful beast known as CHANGE, things are not being done that way anymore around here. Sound familiar?

During times of great change—reorganization, new data systems, strategic planning, downsizing, mergers, relocation and sometimes all of this at once—the actual quality of work takes a nose dive. For people whose internal QC's are modeled after General George Patton, this is a painful time. Yes, everyone knows that tools need to be returned to proper places, files need to be kept perfectly, copy machines need to be maintained—and you know what? with all this change going on, it's probably not going to happen. During these times you need to have a serious chat with your internal Quality Control Director or risk the chance of being driven stark raving mad.

So there are eight characters (or voices or directors) that are most easily recognized in the minds of most people. Every individual has many more "parts" or characters. We seem to have this core group of eight in common.

Exercise 4

At this moment imagine that you are the Statue of Liberty and there are lots of little people looking out through the windows in your crown. All of your internal directors are reading this page right along with you. Some of them are thrilled that you are finally getting this concept because they've been wanting to talk to you for a long time. Some of the others, however, are already feeling threatened and want you to stop reading before you actually start getting control of your life. All of this is OK.

"Hi, it's going to be all right!"

> **"The more you can be aware of
> and communicate with all the parts of yourself,
> the more they will cooperate with you."**
> —Cobar Pita

Let's expand the challenge even more. You have at least eight conflicting voices inside your mind. Your spouse has eight different parts on the inside of their minds. What are the chances that these combined 16 parts are going to match up and agree on every issue? Zero. None. Nada. Zip. You may think you've found your Soul Mate but you will not have a 100% match on every internal director.

If you think you work in a small business, think again. If every employee there represents eight different agendas simultaneously, that makes for a very large crowd. If you think that people are inconsistent, you're right and now you know why.

Who are these directors and how did they get inside your head? HOW they got there is the study of psychology—I don't do that part. The fact that these characters are communicating with you that's communication—I do that part!

Transactional Analysis gave us the Inner Parent, Adult and Child. That was expanded to the Critical Parent, Nurturing Parent and Inner Brat. Popular humor has given us:

"My inner child can beat up your inner child."

"My inner Power Animal is a Pack Rat."

"Her lips tell me no-no but there's yes-yes in her eyes."

"My heart and mind give conflicting signals but the call of my stomach is always clear."

"I wouldn't be broke if the voices in my head paid rent."

"I was at home, alone and in bad company."

"If the Goddess within me doesn't lose 20 pounds, I'm going to have to ask her to leave."

"I killed my inner child and buried him with the others."

"I keep trying to get in touch with my inner child. I'm sending down more peanut butter."

"Get in touch with your Inner Idiot."

"My evil twin did it."

A special notation here about the concept of the Inner Child. Now which one would that be? The sweet brat you were at two years old or the obnoxious teenager you were at 15? Maybe it's the helpful 5-year old? Or the inquisitive 10-year old? What on earth is this Inner "Child" stuff? It's really: Inner Children. Plural. Very plural. The stubborn teenager you used to be didn't go anywhere—they're still in there! The charming toddler you used to be isn't disposable like diapers! All the You's you used to be, they're all still there. And quite a gang they are too.

The combination of all your "parts" is what makes you so incredibly unique—not in just a special spiritual way—but in a practical, concrete communication sort of way. You are absolutely unique, just like everyone else.

I sometimes refer to this collection of parts as the "gang of bandits" because they can't seem to agree on much and they seem to be holding people hostage. Like you.

I told you that this was not without humor.

Right now there is something in your closet (you know what it is) that your Internal PR Director will not let you wear it and your Internal Financial Director will not let you throw it away.

The Goodwill truck is on its way to your neighborhood and you're cleaning out your closet, but there is one item, every year, you push it back into the closet because you "paid too much to give that away."

I heard one seminar participant say, "I've got a whole basement full of stuff like that!"

A Brilliant Observation

A woman participant looked at her internal organizational chart and said, "You know, my husband and I get along really well. There's just one area…"

(Isn't there always?) She continued, "I'm going to have *my* Financial Director write to *his* Financial Director so that the rest of us can go on having a good time together!"

The minute I heard this, I knew it would work. Why involve the entire internal corporation when there's only one part that needs work? She's got it. Do marriage counselors know about this? This is a great idea.

Communicating with Parts

I have had only one client who ever said, "Money is no object." I was hired to help him create the strategic plan for his new company, a land development firm. In the course of one of our conversations, David started talking about cars. This isn't unusual since I'm afflicted with a minor virus known as Car Nut-itis and conversations with me frequently slide over into the subject of cars.

David could afford to buy any car manufactured today. But he couldn't bring himself to buy the car that he lusted for—a Jaguar. Part of David wanted the car and part of David would not allow him to have it.

The thing to remember here is: *I don't care what kind of car David drives.* Makes no difference to me. But what I need here is a CEO with his mind on the strategic plan and his mind is being interrupted by a tug of war over a car!

After the meeting I went back to my office and I called around about Jaguars. I found out how much it would cost to rent a Jaguar for a day, a week and a month. Then I wrote a letter to the Internal Financial Director of David—*not to David* but to the part of David saying "no" to the Jaguar.

You and I both know that if David drives a Jaguar for one week, at the end of that week he will either say, "This is a fantastic car and I must have this car!" or he's going to say, "Hmmmmm. This isn't such a big deal. I don't need this Jaguar."

If you have one part saying, "I want it" (whatever the want is) and another part saying, "You can't have it" —when these parts are fighting with each other—that's self-sabotage. When you lose weight and then gain it back, it is pretty obvious that part of you wants it off and part of you *doesn't.* If you've ever been attracted to someone that you knew was not "good for you," then you've experienced that emotional seesaw. Back and forth.

When this swinging back and forth from "I want it" and "You can't have it" (or you shouldn't have it) stops, we call that serenity or peace of mind.

I wanted David's internal war (over the Jaguar anyway) to cease so that we could use all of his mind to work on the strategic plan. Again, remember it doesn't matter to me what kind of car he drives but I do care about the quality of his concentration. A brain conflicted is only a partial brain. For what we were doing, I wanted as much of his attention as I could get.

Result: We came up with a brilliant mission statement for David's company and the strategic plan almost wrote itself after that. David was driving his Jaguar. Who cares? David's internal parts, that's who cares.

What makes the difference here is a Quality of Life issue. To experience a greater Quality of Life, a person needs self-management skills. That means that you tend to ALL parts of yourself. It means that each part of you needs attention and care and honor. To refuse to acknowledge and honor a part with a need is to court self-sabotage. Jaguars or Pontiacs—makes no difference. What makes a critical difference, however, is the pushing and pulling that goes on in your motivated or unmotivated mind.

There is a segment of research that looks at what happens to you when you stifle an internal character or part. As an example, let's say you have a part inside you that loves to sing. Just for the sheer joy of making music with your throat, you sing. Let's add to the mix that you have a less than beautiful voice and you don't want to put in the time and effort to make it better and you don't really want to alter your lifestyle to become a professional singer.

Because you're not willing to turn pro is *no reason to stop singing*. In fact, you *must* sing. In your shower, in your car, while you putter in the yard, with a church choir. If there is a part of you that needs to sing, then you must sing. If you don't, you'll find yourself, the theory goes, having a lot of sore throats. Some believe that the term "sore throat" is really a misspelled message and that the message is "Soar, throat!" If you have a part that loves to sing and you don't sing, if you don't let your voice soar, then it will sore in other ways.

> **"Desires that are repressed unconsciously**
> **by fear, anxiety and social taboos**
> **can reappear in other guises**
> **such as psychosomatic illnesses."**
> —Ester Schaler Buchholz

If you're homesick for Seattle, a part of you can sabotage your job until you're finally back in Seattle. If you don't honor the part of yourself that wants the weight *on,* then you will wake up in your house with food mysteriously gone—and you're the only one who lives there. If you don't respect that fat teenager you were, the one who couldn't get a date then when you're pursued as an adult, you might find keeping your hands off the intern too much of a temptation. The theory goes that if you need to sculpt or make things with your hands but you spend decades of your life in a paper world, don't be surprised when your hands turn on you and develop an arthritic-like condition.

Why do so many people have heart attacks? Why would a heart *attack* its owner? Is it because the heart has longed for something, has always been denied and then finally "attacks"?

Will ignoring your internal parts actually cause illness? Do I believe this theory? I don't know. You must admit, the play on language is *very* interesting. Doesn't matter. What I *know* is that we need to be good managers of our various selves—good shepherds to our own internal flocks. That *does* make for a healthier mind. We need to honor our quirks and realize that we now have a huge management problem—taking care of all those internal parts. If we ignore them long enough and continue to procrastinate, they don't sit quietly. They leak out in amazing ways. They will eventually get what they want even if they sabotage the whole to get it.

If you've wanted to get involved with music in any way, I suggest you get started. People who have energetically made it to their 100th birthdays frequently play a musical instrument. Research indicates that music requires simultaneous reading, listening, memorizing and using manual skills. This produces multiple benefit for the brain and includes the ability to resist trauma and illness. Music has been shown to reduce the negative impacts of stress. If the only thing you've ever played is the radio, sign up for lessons to learn to play a musical instrument.

Which is exactly what I'm going to do if I ever get this book finished. I have the guy's business card and if he's still alive, I'm taking accordion lessons.

If you have something inside you that wants to make its own music, you owe it to yourself to give it your time.

Imagine what you could accomplish if you could meet and negotiate with those people who are really running your life— not all the people on the *outside* of you, but all the people on the *inside*. That's who's really running your life. When you tend to all parts of yourself, the self-sabotaging behavior ends.

Chapter 4
The Course—Part II

**"What a gift of grace to be able
to take the chaos from within
and from it create
some semblance of order."**
—Katherine Paterson

So, as it turns out, you now have a huge management challenge. You are the president of the corporation known as YourSelf, Inc. And you have many vice-presidents that report to you on various aspects of your company, your life. These parts, when not in agreement, cause the phenomenon known as self-sabotage.

How well run is your company? Are your projects on time (procrastination)? Or on budget (financial sabotage)? When you give your internal staff an order, do they get it done for you? Can you pick a weight for your company and then weigh it?

Here's a typical meeting in an American corporation:
Marketing says, "This is the way to go."
Research and Development says, "This is the way to go."
PR says, "This is the way to go."
Manufacturing says, "This is the way to go."
and Finance says, "No" to everything.

But there are some companies where all the vice-presidents *agree* on what needs to be done and how it should be done. It is as if they're hooked up to the same plow and headed in the same direction. We call these "excellent" companies and we write books about them. If you have a company like this, Tom Peters will come camp on your door step and write articles about you.

Now take that parallel into the concept that each person has a corporation within them.

When you describe someone as "self-directed" or seems to have "self-confidence" or they're "very focused" or "know what they want," you know what that says to me? It tells me that all or *enough* of their internal parts or vice-presidents *agree* on what they need to be doing and they do it! This internal agreement causes *consistent behavior.* Consistent behavior is required to accomplish most goals.

If everyone on the inside of you agreed to write a book, what would we have a year from now?

We'd have a book!

"Doubt is the result of conflicting wishes.
Be sure of what you want
and doubt becomes impossible."
—*A Course in Miracles*

Ah! "Conflicting wishes"! That's as short and perfect a description as I have found to describe the cause of self-sabotage. Unfortunately we're the last to know what our own conflicting wishes are. We only hear one side of it because we can't or won't hear the conflicting side. We think we know ourselves and what we want but when we watch our actions, we get a different story. Unbeknownst to us there is a "higher need" within us.

If you suddenly came across an accident scene and found a stranger in need of immediate medical attention, you would go into action. If you had a cell phone, you'd use it. If there was bleeding you'd find something to wrap the wound even if you had to remove your own shirt to do it. If the person were conscious, you'd comfort them with reassuring words.

You would NOT:
- start to place a 911 call and then say, "Oh, we might be disturbing someone, maybe I shouldn't call."
- attempt to stop the bleeding and then say, "You know, you're genetically programmed to bleed so maybe you should just bleed."

- berate the person for being in this predicament…"what did you do to get yourself in this stupid mess?"

Why would we treat a stranger in need better than we would treat ourselves? Fascinating question. And what's even more remarkable, strangers, finding us in similar peril, would take better care of us than we do of ourselves!

When you say you want something and then don't do it, that means that part of you wants it and part of you *doesn't* want it. You start to tackle your self-imposed assignment and then, for some reason, you sabotage yourself. I believe that the "reason," if you knew it, is a Very Good Reason. Your sabotaging behavior is a message from some part of you that wants something. The message is written in code. Your job is to crack the code.

"Know thyself."

Well, you didn't come with an instruction manual! Be nice if you had one. I don't know of any better or easier way to get to know yourself than having an Internal Theatre system in place.

If you're sabotaging something in your life, these "conflicting wishes" of yours need to meet and negotiate. The dictionary defines *negotiate* as "to confer with another so as to arrive at the settlement of some matter, to arrange for or bring about through conference, discussion and compromise."

FAQ: "How do you negotiate with the characters inside your head?"

If countries are going to negotiate an arms treaty or companies are going to negotiate a labor contract, what's the first thing they have to agree to? They have to agree on a place. And the second thing? Establish rapport.

When you honor and respect the parts of yourself, you establish rapport and become confidants and then, of course, you're able to *influence yourself*. (Isn't it remarkable the amount of information available about influencing other people? And yet, wouldn't it be great if we could just influence ourselves?)

The Inner Theatre Method

1. The setting.

Create a place in your imagination/mind where you will do your "work," the work of processing dilemmas, questions, purchases, behavioral changes, everything from writer's block to losing weight. This setting needs:

a) comfortable spot for You—an overstuffed chair, a throne, whatever suits you on center stage.

b) suitable room for your parts, your directors, your vice-presidents. Something like a theatre setting works well, a grandstand with bleachers, a palladium, a ball room. It's all yours, create what you want. Your spot is center stage, whether you're in your own personal Madison Square Garden or a small, intimate dinner theatre arrangement. Seating for the audience is the seating for your inner parts. Create this space with the idea that the internal parts can also communicate with other parts as well as with you.

2. The method.

Three ways to use this method:

...get quiet and listen to the dialogue.

...have a friend/therapist lead you through a negotiation.

...write it. (More on this later.)

Writing has the advantage of: you have a written record (minutes of the meeting) and can go back over it; you will stay on track (less mind-wandering); writing has been shown to improve health; written dialogues look like scripts.

Example:

Here you are in the health section of your favorite grocery store with your list from *Prevention Magazine* of all the vitamins and supplements needed to maintain a healthy body...

HD (Health Director): "Let's see, Vitamin E..."

FD (Financial Director): "That's $10."

HD: "Vitamin B-12 complex..."

FD: "That's $8.50."

HD: "Calcium."

FD: "That's $12!"

HD: "Ginkgo."

FD: "Seven bucks!"

HD: "We need all this to be healthy!"

FD: "Put that stuff back—we're not going to be the healthiest person in the poor house!"

You: "Well, here's Centrum. It's only $10 and it's probably got everything in it anyway."

HD: "There's no ginkgo in it."

FD: "There's things you don't need to remember anyway."

What's just happened here? A little compromise. And these compromises are occurring all day long within You. Some take only nano seconds to complete. They happen so fast that you are not aware of them.

Writing also has the advantage of slowing down the dialogue to a pace that you can become aware of it. When you write, send your Internal Copy Editor out for a well-deserved break. While you are doing this work you don't need to care about crossing your t's, proper spelling or paragraph breaks. Just get it out and onto paper!

3. The process: Opening a dialogue.

Talking to a character who has no stake in the issue is like phoning a wrong number. Depending on what issue you chose, there will be some parts who are vitally interested in the issue and some that don't care about the issue. It is important that you speak to the most appropriate part. (If you're working on a weight issue, for instance, don't ask to speak to the Health Director—if they were in charge, you'd weigh a perfect weight, wouldn't you? Instead you need to speak to "the person in charge of my weight.")

You may experience a little "static on the line" at first. This may occur when you attempt contact with an internal part that has been controlling an issue for you a long time (such as weight). This internal part has a great deal of power and they are winning. Why should they want to talk with You?

> **"When we ignore a part of ourselves, this is just as irritating as when someone we know ignores us.**
> **Ignore it long enough and it will create problems until it gets our attention with its message."**
> —Cobar Pita

Someone who has been winning, remember, is a winner and deserves your respect. Your initial feeling about this part may be: *if I get my hands on 'em, I'm gonna throttle 'em!*

This is not a great way to enter a negotiation. Don't go to the Internal Theatre with the attitude of kicking butt. These are your Survival Mechanisms and they have done a superior job of taking care of you. You've made it *this* far. Your parts love you and they have your survival as their goal. They have a Very Good Reason for doing what they do. Quirky reasons, perhaps, but good reasons. They have a higher need. Trust this.

At first you may believe that there can be no possible "good reason" for this sabotage because there is so much information contrary to this idea. What possible benefit could there be in being 100 pounds overweight? Everyone can tell you that it's not healthy.

I can think of lots of benefits to being overweight. Some of them are valid and some are just perceived. To an internal part, however, they are valid *period*. (If you can't come up with benefits to being overweight, for example, then you're not tapped into being creative yet. See Step 6.)

Parts in your Inner Theatre may be male, female, animal, vegetable, mineral, cartoon, famous people, relatives and even just balls of light. You don't have to direct this. There is no right or wrong experience here (where else can you go for such a delightful time?). Your personal internal Financial Director may or may not wear a 3-piece suit. Your internal Health Director may not be wearing jogging shorts. Lighten up. Take what you get.

When you have your theatre pictured, say: "I want to work on the issue of _____ (fill in the blank). I want to speak to the part who is in charge of _____. Would that person be willing to stand up?"

When the part identifies themselves, *thank them.* "Thank you for identifying yourself. Would you be willing to speak with me about this issue?"

Do not ask "why" questions. A "why" question is usually not a question at all but a statement or a thinly disguised judgment call. State your question in a different way. "Of what benefit are you to me?" OR "You've been with me a long time. You must be very important. What pay value are you interested in?"

Every internal part is a Survival Mechanism and is there for your *survival.* They feel protective of their mission. Protection against what? Well, this is a scary planet and we have lots of things to fear both real and imagined. When it comes to how your internal parts operate, there is no such thing as an irrational fear. It's all rational and justified. What appears to be illogical at first, is *quite* logical when the Very Good Reason is known. There are no set formulas here. You find your own way.

"Life is a personal event."
—Alan Urbach

$4.$ Guidelines.

What do you do if you want to speak to a part that doesn't respond to you?

This isn't AT&T. If this were a phone line and you couldn't get through, what would you do? You'd switch to a mode of communicating that doesn't involve a phone line. You'd write. That's exactly what you would do here too. You'd would get paper and pen and find a quiet place and begin your dialogue.

Don't be surprised if you encounter resistance. This may be due to a variety of things. Can you guess what they might be?

a) the Very Good Reason may be highly protected, very personal and the Survival Mechanism feels that you can't handle the truth of what the good reason is. (Remember Jack Nicholson as the testifying military man in *A Few Good Men?*)

b) the Survival Mechanism doesn't trust you. Is there any reason why they should? In order to get past this one, you can demonstrate your trustworthiness to another part first. For instance, make a commitment to your health or your finances, engage in a mutually beneficial negotiation, honor that commitment and the other parts will make note of it...and be more willing to open up to you.

c) an internal part may be unwilling to communicate because they think you're going to ridicule them or try to talk them out of how they think or feel without taking care of their needs.

"The point in knowing your internal parts is just that: knowing them. By knowing them, you know yourself."
—Cobar Pita

You are not interested in changing them. To honor all of You, you also uncover the parts of you that you have ignored or hidden.

5. Continuing the dialogue.

Practice the phrase "would you be willing...?" These are the words of a skilled negotiator. Negotiate peaceful settlements within yourself.

Examples:

"Would you be willing to work with me on this issue?"

"Would you be willing to take off 3 pounds? 1 pound?"

"Would you be willing to go without sugar for 10 minutes?"

"Would you be willing to help me write just a first draft?"

"Would you be willing to do this until April?"

"Would you be willing to be uncomfortable for a few days?"

"Would you be willing to just look up the phone number?"

"Would you be willing to collect the information—even if we don't go?"

"Wouldn't it be great if you could talk to yourself...and really mean it?"

6. Ask, "Of what benefit are you to me?"

or

"What higher need do you serve (that I don't know about)?"

7. GET CREATIVE.

When your internal part lets you know what their Very Good Reason is behind their motivation (example: having extra weight on as a protection from the return of a bout with cancer)...

a) accept it.

Cardinal Rule: Do not attempt to talk this part into some other way of thinking, feeling or believing. This is an incredible waste of time, effort, energy and besides, it's insulting. Accept what they say, no matter how illogical it may seem to you at the time. Saying, "you shouldn't feel that way" to anyone (inside you or outside you) will only escalate a problem. Instead, acknowledge it. Then work with that.

b) agree to honor whatever the benefit is.

Now you can begin brainstorming solutions. You can:

a) come up with *other ways* to get that benefit.

b) ask for a temporary postponement of the benefit. (Include a date.)

Examples:

"I discovered that the reason I couldn't finish writing the story was because I was afraid of what my mother would think if she ever read it."

"I learned that the reason I have the weight on is to drive my spouse away! She says that my extra weight is not attractive and what I'm saying back to her is that there are things about her that I don't think are attractive either. There are other ways of handling this problem and I'm going to find them."

"The reason I wouldn't let myself earn more money is because I didn't want to distance myself from my lower income parents and relatives. They always said, 'Don't get too big for your britches.'"

"I discovered that the reason I couldn't be thin is because I would lose my group of friends. They'd hate me. We are a sociopolitical group and ridiculing 'normal weight' women is part of our pattern. I hate to admit it, but if I'm thin, they wouldn't confide in me."

"I put off things at the office until the last minute for one great and delicious reason: I like the adrenaline rush. I like becoming the center of the fire storm. It's beginning to wear on my staff, however. I need to find other ways to get this feeling without involving my co-workers."

These are all real examples from real people who didn't have a choice about their behavior until they created a space (theatre) in their imagination/minds for their inner parts to express themselves. The average time discovering these major obstructing patterns took less than 15 minutes.

It is useful to ask, "How can I take care of the higher need, the Very Good Reason in another way? How can I give myself the same benefit, but in another way, a way I'd find more useful."

As a practice, before starting your own discovery, you could go back over the 5 examples above and counsel these people. How would you advise the writer to finish the story? How would you satisfy the person who gets an adrenaline rush at the office? When your own inner parts watch you being a good advisor and negotiate settlements where the parts are honored, they will automatically begin to trust you.

Contemplating leaving your job and starting a business? And every day you change your mind? You need to ask, what would have to be in place for me to feel comfortable starting my own business? Then write the list. Put everything on the list that you'd prefer to have in place. Go back over the list and check what you absolutely *have to have*.

When asked, your internal parts know exactly what would have to be in place before it would be OK for you to start your own business. If you ask them, they will tell you. Write it down. It may be a terribly farfetched list but at least you now know what it is. (Your next question might be, "How long would it take to get everything on this list?")

In the marvelous book *Wishcraft,* the author Barbara Sher suggests that you also create a list of all the reasons your project can't be done. For instance, list all the reasons why it isn't possible for you to lose 5 pounds. Perhaps your lifestyle has dictated that you eat half your meals away from home. You eat on planes, in your car, at business lunches and client dinners. Is this a solvable dilemma? What suggestions would you make to someone that has this challenge?

Notice that when I ask you to solve a problem for "someone with this challenge" *you can come up with solutions!* You can *rapidly* come up with solutions. Yet these are the same challenges that end up on your Whine List.

Writers' Block? Frequently, perfection is the obstacle. If that's it, then give yourself permission to do it *imperfectly.* Don't try to get it right, *get it written.* Any commitment to something that results in growth will probably unnerve you. So my next question would be, "Would you be willing to be frightened for a little while in order to get what you want?"

People are astonished to discover that they can say "yes" to this question. When the fears have been kept beneath the surface and not acknowledged, they are huge, *unsurmountable.* But when they are told to you and listed on paper and when that magical question is asked, people suddenly have courage.

8. Gratitude.

Thank your internal part for:
 a) identifying themselves.
 b) for being there for you.
 c) for the care and protection they have given you.
 d) for sharing their information.
 e) for agreeing to be creative about solutions.

9. Agree to renegotiate.

Influencing yourself will improve when you promise your internal character-in-charge that, at a future time you agree to update and examine how things are going and that you are open to renegotiate.

If you lose 60 pounds and your life turns into a giant mess and you truly believe that your new slender form is the reason, and *you can't come up with a creative way to handle it,* then you'd better go have another conversation. FAST.

If your career takes off, leaving your spouse frightened and confused, probably time to have an additional conversation about your priorities. If you want to *have it all,* state that to yourself and then come up with solutions. You may have invested heavily in your career because you wanted a great career or you may have invested heavily in your career solely because you knew it was a way out of your spousal relationship.

> **"I think a lot of people are at war**
> **with themselves inside. They think they**
> **want to be out there but there's a part of them**
> **that doesn't."**
> —T. Duncan

Your internal characters will work for you if they feel that you really will listen and be open to renegotiate in the future.

Example:

(to the Internal Fat Person) "Would you be willing to put up with the comments of 'well-meaning' friends, while I experience being thin?" Your loving Internal Fat Person may say, *"Sure! But how exactly are you going to handle it when they say, 'Oh, one little bite won't hurt! Go ahead and treat yourself'?"*

(to the Internal People Pleaser) "Would you be willing to be uncomfortable while I work on my assertiveness skills?" *The reply may be: "Work on your assertiveness skills with whom?"*

(to the Internal Social Director) "Would you be willing to postpone getting together with friends until I get three chapters of my book written?" *The response may be: "I'll wipe the calendar free of friends but I'm not giving up any time with the grandchildren!"*

(to the Internal Clean Freak) "Would you be willing to tolerate a less than perfectly clean house until I get the taxes done?" *Your Clean Freak may answer: "Dust is OK but no dirty dishes in the sink."*

(to the Internal Shopper) "Would you be willing to avoid the mall until the credit cards are paid off?" *And the response may be: "How long will that take?"*

(to the Internal Car Nut) "Would you be willing to forego buying a new car for two years until our retirement goal is met?" *Don't be surprised if your Internal Car Nut says, "Sure, providing we don't run across a '59 Caddie convertible for less than $20,000. I mean, be reasonable. I'm not a saint!"*

Got the idea?

10. Closing.

You will never meet more fascinating people than the people who live on the inside of your head. Television will be boring compared to the conversations you'll have.

Go with an Attitude of Gratitude: always thank the parts for communicating with you! They have the power, otherwise you wouldn't be reading this, so bring a lot of respect. And humor *helps*.

TIPS FOR THE INNER THEATRE: 4 Additional Techniques

Create a list of people you'd go to for advice if you could or people *who solve problems in a way that you historically haven't*. Take a moment and write the names of these people:

_____   _____

_____   _____

_____   _____

_____   _____

If you get stuck looking for a solution, ask: "What would _____ do if they had this problem?"

What *would* Gen. George Patton do if he had your situation? What would I'll-never-go-hungry-again Scarlet

O'Hara do? How would George Burns have handled this? How about Winnie the Pooh? I know it sounds funny, but when you ask questions like this, you can imagine answers. And getting an answer, any kind of an answer, means you're no longer stuck.

(As I write today, my mind is mulling over a three-quarter scale 1934 Woody wagon replicar that I wanted to buy on Saturday. I think of the car fondly and know that Gen. George Patton probably wouldn't have thought much of this California beach bum plastic car. And if I consider the advice of Scarlet O'Hara, I see the wisdom of leaving my money in the bank and the car behind. When I think of George Burns, I see George with his cigar, shrugging his classic shrug because he doesn't care one way or the other. When I wonder what Winnie the Pooh would have done, I can see that funny little car in my driveway. This process took less than a minute. It was an enjoyable exercise for my mind to do and I end by asking myself, "So you want Winnie the Pooh running your life this week?" I chuckle to myself and my mind clears and I'm able to go back to work. See, that's how it works!)

Another technique…

Once you have brainstormed some possible solutions for yourself, ask: What am I willing to do *today* or for the next hour? for the next 5 minutes?"

Think about it. You don't have to lose 60 pounds or even 10 pounds. You only have to lose ONE. And even that one pound is 16 one-ounce pieces. You don't have to write an entire book. You don't have to write 250 pages or 110 pages. Just ONE page. Just ONE word. If you're trying to break a habit that involves a temptation (sexual or smoking or gambling or eating, for example) can you put it off for 5 minutes? Can you go 10 minutes without it? Most people respond to this by saying, "Of course." Well, that's all you have to do for now.

If you think you're such a great procrastinator, then exercise your procrastinator muscle. If you put off doing your taxes, why not put off eating a cookie?

Another technique…

Ask yourself: What will happen if I am successful?

At having money. At writing. At being thin. At being creative. At being more organized. At being a success. Whatever it is for you, vividly imagine yourself completely successful. Create all the visual detail of that scene for yourself. Take two minutes and project yourself into this successful picture.

Stop reading and make the imagination/mind pictures. Stop reading now.

Now imagine that you are completely on target with your projected success and you are at a party. How do people react to you? Do they ask you for technical advice? Do they bring you problems? Do they ignore you? Do they "hit you up" for things? Do they seem sincere? Is everybody friendly? Do they offer you food, advice or the door? How is the world treating you?

One successful business woman did this exercise and realized that she thought that if she had a million dollars that she would have to dress like a middle aged matron and drive a Mercedes sedan. She prefers sweatsuits and her Jeep. You and I both know that she can wear and drive anything she wants. However, if her picture of herself as a millionaire is one that she regards as a negative picture, she's going to have a more difficult time convincing her internal parts to go along with this success picture. She "rewrote" her picture of what a millionaire looks like and ended her two-year sabotage of her finances.

If you become successful at getting whatever it is you want, what person or persons in your life wouldn't like it? If you got what you wanted, you might be alienated from someone or some group. What does that look like to you? And are you willing to accept it?

Another technique…

Imagine that you have not succeeded and you're happy about that. What?! Take two minutes and vividly imagine that you are not at all in your success picture and what does that look like for you?

Stop reading and vividly imagine this scene. If it involves acquiring something, then you didn't get it. If it involves a behavioral habit, imagine that you are actually worse off than you are now. Example, if you're 60 pounds overweight, imagine that you're 100 pounds overweight. If you're $5,000 in debt, imagine that you're $200,000 in debt. If you smoke, imagine that you do not stop all day long, you light one cigarette with a burning cigarette. In order to do this exercise correctly, you must imagine in detail what it feels like for you.

How do people react to this form of You? Are they friendlier or do they ignore you? And do you like that more or less? Are they sympathetic or do they ask for your advice? Are you comfortable with that? To they share their feelings more openly or do they show you to the door? Are you welcomed? Do they share things with you or offer to care for you? How are things different?

People can make startling discoveries about themselves and how they perceive others *perceiving them* with this exercise. Do it. Take two minutes and see yourself further away from your success picture than you've ever been.

One woman who had always held her weight problem in check vividly imagined herself obese and at a party. She had a great time in her imagination and realized that as a heavy woman she could flirt outrageously and no one would take her seriously. It was great fun in her mind. She also felt that she would have to be nicer to people and they, in turn would be nice to her too. At a normal weight she could allow herself to be assertive but as a very overweight woman she didn't feel that she could allow herself to be both fat and assertive. But, also in her mind, no one took her seriously on career matters either. This mental exercise startled her. She didn't know that these perceptions were strongly held by her internal parts. After vividly seeing this picture she no longer had to white knuckle herself with her food plan. Without harranging herself, she began walking the stairs in her office building and found herself in front of a stationery bicycle at a garage sale. The vividly imagined party exercise had subtly changed her. "I don't want to have to pretend to be jolly when I'm not," she said. "That would really, really bother me to have to put myself under that kind of pressure." She's been on that bike toning up ever since.

**"She tires easily under the
pressure to be interesting."**
—the character Niles Crane describing Maris
on an episode of "Frazier"

Other Ah-ha's and Shared Experiences

Mike discovered that by procrastinating on his taxes he was able to be the center of attention with his family every April. The quiet of his study was uninterrupted except for offers of his favorite foods. Tax preparation for Mike was the source of much drama and in a busy household it provided him with the solitude he craved and a perfect excuse not to participate in playing taxi service for his children. Tax preparation occurs every year, same time, no surprises. Mike had a higher need that was met by procrastinating.

Gregarious Bill was successful with his 70 pound weight loss until he walked into a familiar crowd and no one recognized him. Always the one to enjoy and joke with people, Bill was devastated. Without his awareness, an inner part of Bill gained the weight back for him and this jolly fat man is now recognized and welcomed. He had a higher need to be recognized than a need to be thin. He's also now suffering from foot and back problems. Bill has just discovered what his weight is doing for him and is beginning to come up with a creative strategy for dealing with it. His weight problem will eventually shorten his life and, as Bill puts it, "I don't need to be a corpse that people recognize."

Jim sabotaged his job to the point that he was nearly fired. His Very Good Reason, of course, was that he was homesick for Seattle and needed his wife's support for his desire to move back there. Going back home served a higher need for Jim than being a good employee.

**"Once the subconscious mind accepts an idea,
it begins to execute it."**
—Joseph Murphy

A young musician and his friend were both visiting Oahu, Hawaii for the first time and they were having lunch at the Kahala Hilton. There were hundreds of orchids in the lobby, a dolphin tank, turtle pools, an elaborate buffet and a Japanese wedding taking place on the lush lawn next to the beach front. The young man seemed intimidated by the lavish surroundings. "I don't think we belong here," he commented. "You may not belong here," said his companion, "but I sure as hell do. If you're not comfortable in a beautiful place like this, you'll never have the money you say you want."

Pamela knew full well, once she vividly imagined herself thin, that her husband would not like it. She decided to lose the weight anyway, watched and listened as he made every effort to sabotage her efforts, did what she could in couples counseling and after she took off 100 pounds, it was OK with Pamela to lose another 180 pounds (her husband). Losing the weight served a higher need in Pamela than being married to that particular man.

"Remember, in all our misery, we are comfortable."
—Wally Minto

People really are getting what they want. If they complain about it, it's giving them something to complain about. If it seems insane that a person would carry an extra 100 pounds, it might be because they know what problems it would cause if they lost it. If it seems crazy that a person keeps making bad financial decisions, it might keep them close to their low income roots. The mystery is figuring out what it is that you really, really want. What higher need is being served here? Somebody on the inside wants something and they want it for a Very Good Reason. Your job is to discover the reason and give yourself that benefit without the use of the sabotage.

Your behavior is a coded message from some part of you that wants something. Your job is to crack this code.

Allison had called it quits with her married lover six times in the past six weeks. The drama of it all was beginning to bore even Allison who had a great capacity for enduring it. She didn't want to be the Other Woman but she didn't want to refuse her lover in the process. Many of us, in an effort to be Nice Guys or Good Sports, sacrifice an inner goal. On what seemed to be a whim, Allison posed nude for an art class. When she displayed one of the sketches to her paramour, he was outraged and stormed out of her life permanently. Allison felt an usual sense of relief as he drove away, a feeling she hadn't anticipated. It took a couple of days before she realized that unconsciously she had created this situation and that some part of her had masterminded it. Allison, consciously unable to find the courage, had tried "reasoning" with herself. Obviously one of her internal parts decided to solve her problem for her. Even Allison could find the humor in a man who objected to her posing for an art class but accepted his own adultery.

So it turns out, that your Survival Mechanisms have been playing an excellent part in your life; they've been efficient, always alert and steadfast. You may think you want something but there's a part that's holding you back.

> **"Is how people change**
> **one of the most important questions**
> **we could ask in the whole history of humanity?**
> **You change when you serve the real need**
> **of the voice that's stopping you."**
> —T. Duncan

And you want to know something really radical? Change is just that simple. Not easy. But simple.

Chapter 5
The Course—Part III

**"I cannot count the good people I know
who would be even better
if they bent their spirits
to the study of their own hungers."**
—M.F.K. Fisher

The most difficult decisions you have to make involve: staying and going.

This is pretty obvious when we're talking about a job or a relationship. Expand the way you think of staying and going. It could also mean remodeling your house, trying a new hair style or color, foreign travel, dental or cosmetic surgery or even getting a pet. Should you stay with your situation the way that it is now or should you go into the new challenge?

Staying and going issues turn your Inner Theatre into a political convention. All parts have an issue with your issue and they're vocal. You're trying to decide if you want to remain *status quo* (stay) or go for it.

"Listen to the still, small voice within."

"A still, small voice." Ah, if it were only *one*. But it isn't. I don't get a "still, small voice," I get a chorus and so do you! As you listen, it's as if a tennis ball is loose inside a clothes dryer. Your decision-making is complicated by a barrage of advice and concerns. If you get opinions from friends or colleagues outside yourself, it multiplies the scope.

The reason you find it so difficult to start your own business, leave a partner or even dye your hair is because you're not sure that you're going to be happy with the decision. Six months from now will you say, *"What* did I do that for?" or will you say, "Wow! I wish I'd done this sooner!"

Will I regret it? Like a banner stretched across the ceiling of your imagination/mind, these words keep you from making a decision. For many issues, if you wait long enough, a decision will be made for you.

Both the dentist and the car mechanic use the line "You can pay me now" (for a minor repair) or "You can pay me later" (when it gets to be major).

"To not decide is to decide."

Yes, I've decided, I'm going to do it. Next day, no, I'm sure I'm not going to do this. Back and forth. Some people have suggested that they just take a vote every day for a month and at the end of 30 days the majority wins. The only problem with that is: how many times during the day will you take the vote?

Eventually you may hear an inner part say, "You are so indecisive! Can't you just make a decision?" Fat lot of good that comment is!

"Those inner voices? I wake up in the morning, the jury's in and I'm guilty!"
—Lynn Easton

Now, however, you're equipped with the best possible tool for making faster decisions and decisions you'll want to live with. Now you have the Inner Theatre system in place and that's where you'll do your work.

Instead of groaning to yourself every time you hear another piece of conflicting advice in your mind, manage it. Self-management is the opposite of self-sabotage.

How does a good manager make a decision?

A good manager will listen to advice, sort out what's relevant, set a time limit and arrive at a decision. Some will use the Einstein method of turning the decision over to the subconscious mind and expect (and get!) a decision when they wake up in the morning. To prevent "analysis paralysis" a good manager understands that he/she will never have *all the information they would like to have* about a situation and know that they will make a decision anyway. They also seem to trust that they will have internal resources to deal with whatever happens because of their decision. They are willing to accept responsibility for their decisions. That's why they get the big bucks.

Skills involving managing people are transferable to your inner imagination/mind, your Inner Theatre. If you've had management training courses, that information works with the parts of your Self too. You wouldn't berate staff for their opinions. You'd honor them…after all, you hired them. The same is true for the work you'll do in self-management.

Gather the diverse and conflicting opinions and *hear them out*. Listen and hear the entire pitch from every part. Do not interrupt. Do take notes. When you think you've heard everything and written it all down in front of you, ask if there is anyone else in your Inner Theatre who has an opinion on this issue. Be silent and wait. It's rare that at least one more voice, one more tape doesn't play when given the opportunity. The most shy member of your staff may have the most intelligent thing to tell you. The same is true for your inner voices.

> **"It is those who have a deep and real**
> **inner life who are best able**
> **to deal with the irritating details of outer life."**
> —Evelyn Underhill

The beauty of this system is: now that you know what's there, you may actually find a solution that satisfies every part. That's a big challenge for some issues but before, when your mind was in tennis ball mode, you didn't have a choice. Now, with it all spread out before you, now you have a chance. As a good manager, your inclination should be to see if there is some way to meet all needs. That would be ideal.

If this isn't possible and compromise is inevitable, switch to the phrase "would you be willing?" in communicating with conflicting views. A part that isn't going to get their way would respond well to a time frame. "Would you be willing to support this decision until May?" "I'd like to try this for six months and then take another look at it and I need agreement from all parts." This kind of conversation is positive and virtually eliminates sabotaging.

Let's see how this works in practice. Let's take a life and watch a person trying to make a decision.

Jane

Jane has a steady, 9 to 5 job with medical and dental insurance. Her job is close to her home and she has had this job for over 5 years. Jane is married and has two children. On most days Jane likes her job but more and more often she finds that she tolerates her job.

The issue before Jane is: should she stay with her job or start her own business? Jane has decided and re-decided this issue about 400 times. If we could enter Jane's Inner Theatre we might hear from four different parts of Jane.

Jane's Voice of Reason wears a grey business suit and appreciates good organization. This part of Jane wants market research, flow charts, regional studies and a business plan. This part worries about financial ruin, needs a plan B, C and D and wonders how the bank will accept the idea of this new business venture. Note that all the concerns of this part are valid and sensible.

Another part of Jane is concerned about how the demands of a business enterprise will affect her effectiveness as a mother and wife. Jane strives for perfection on her home front in meal planning and making a comfortable, Norman Rockwell/Martha Stewart home including growing roses. This part argues for family values and mirrors the current media frenzy against people who "want to have it all." This part consoles Jane that what she already has "isn't so bad." This is also the charming part of Jane that doesn't know about business but is willing to put that charm into making a business work.

There is a distraught inner child part of Jane that does not want to grow up and face adult decisions and responsibilities. This part longs for a simpler life of naps and blankies and having the care and protection of someone else. This part is endearing and honest and causes Jane to tire of the whole issue. As a result, when she hears this part, she puts the idea away for another time.

Enter Jane's Gutsy Self who announces that she is going to go ballistic if she doesn't start getting her way pretty soon. This is the fearless Jane that we all want to be...sometimes. She is forceful and funny and tells Jane that the bank, after all, needs *her*. This part is tired of Jane playing Second Banana to what everyone around her wants. She has her own wants and feels that she is creative enough to meet any challenge. She knows that there is talent and internal resources that Jane hasn't even tapped yet.

OK, you're a career counselor and this woman has just walked into *your* office. What do you do with her?

If Jane continues as she has been what is likely to happen? Resentments, if nothing else. She may start to resent her husband, her children and her job. If she continues even longer she will eventually wake up tired and then complain of lack of energy. Many people stay in this stage for years. Or she may slide further into stage three which means she may start coming down with undiagnosable ailments.

If she goes into business, what kind of business should she go into? Well, she's got a death grip on those kids so anything that takes her out of town for long periods of time is probably not a good idea. She is a sociable person so having a work life that requires a constant solitary effort, while perfect for some people, wouldn't work for Jane. She likes answers to her questions before she acts and this is a plus for a wannabe entrepreneur.

In order to experience any peace of mind Jane is going to have to tend to all four parts, satisfy all four. Self-management means tending to *all* parts.

What if Jane owned a business growing roses? You can run the numbers on that one for the accountant side of Jane. This satisfies her other factions too without sacrificing what she holds dearest. This is what happens when a person "finds their passion" or "follows their bliss." It means that enough internal parts are satisfied with this plan and won't sabotage the effort.

When this happens, people find themselves in love with their lives and their projects. They wake up at 4:30 A.M. and can't wait to get started. They say things like, "I'd do this even if I didn't get paid for it" and "Do what you love and you'll never have to work another day in your life."

**"It is the soul's duty to be loyal to its own desires.
It must abandon itself to its master passion."**
—Rebecca West

Self-sabotage is when these internal voices are fighting each other. You become very effective when they stop fighting each other. If other people talked to you the way you talk to yourself, you'd sue! We're rough on ourselves, usually very critical, not much supporting language going on and conflicts are not consciously resolved.

What good is all of this? "It's interesting, but..."

Have you ever sabotaged your career? Do you work next to someone who is sabotaging their career? How about New Year's Resolutions: stop smoking? lose weight? save money? exercise? Where is your resolve by February 1?

The reason will power doesn't work is that there is no *agreement!* In order to come up with a New Year's Resolution, all you need is 51% of the vote! If 51% of your internal parts say "Stop smoking" then you write that resolution. But is 51% *enough* to actually make it happen? For something as challenging as smoking, probably not. You'll need the support of more than just 51% in order to pull this one off. If everyone on the inside agreed to quit smoking, however, that would be *it*.

**"Whether we realize it or not,
there's a good reason behind everything we do
or don't do, every choice we make or avoid."**
—Sarah Ban Breathnach in *Simple Abundance*

We appear to be complex, inconsistent, often irrational, self-defeating and confused. We do not understand why we lose weight and gain it back. We start projects and never finish. We intend to do "good works" and never seem to get to it. In short, we are an unfathomable puzzle to ourselves.

What can be gained by a dialogue with your Internal Directors is understanding about what motivates you. Instead of making no sense, you will begin to see that you make a lot of sense. Your directors, if allowed to speak to you, will tell you why you do what you do.

Whatever your reasons are, a conversation with your internal directors will provide you with information that allows you to "know thyself."

You have read some of the things other people hear in their minds and some of what I hear in mine. Wouldn't you like to meet the parts of You who are really running your life?

It is impossible to do this exercise incorrectly. All you have to do is get quiet and listen. Don't try to direct it. Just take what you get.

Your Turn

I am going to give you the "job title" for three different internal parts or directors. Your mind will actually work faster than you can read. When you read the title of the director, let your eyes leave the page and keep going to the right. Settle your gaze on anything in your environment. And listen for the response.

If this person were
sitting in front of you RIGHT NOW,
what is the one thing your
Financial Director
would have to say to You?⇨⇨⇨⇨

Did you get a pat on the back from the Financial Director? Or did you get yelled at?

Or did you get a little pep talk…a kind of "you could do better if you tried" sort of speech?

Was there anger? Frustration?

Did you get a gold star? Or the Fickle Finger of Fate?

Is your Internal Financial Director a version of Attila the Hun? Or Attila the Ho-Hum?

Let's pick another internal Director. Again, read the director's title and then let your eyes follow off the page and settle in a de-focused way. Listen for the internal response.

If this person were
sitting in front of you RIGHT NOW,
what is the one thing your
Health Director
would have to say to You?⇨ ⇨ ⇨ ⇨

Did you get an "atta boy" from your internal Health Director?

Or did you get scolded?

Did you get the "sandwich" critique: "You're doing this well—YOU NEED TO WORK ON THIS—and you're doing OK on this."

Does your Health Director seem to be well-rooted in Quality of Life for You?

How media-driven is your Health Director? Did you get the feeling that your health is being measured against a standard that's based on what you hear on the evening news?

Or is your Health Director concerned about serious issues that are potentially lethal? Were you advised to make an appointment for a health test: cholesterol? mammogram? blood pressure? colon? If you did, then stop reading, put this book down and go make the appointment NOW.

Just do it.

And now for the last one. Let your eyes follow the arrows off the page, settle on a fixed object. Listen for the internal response.

If this person were
sitting in front of you RIGHT NOW,
what is the one thing your
PR (Public Relations) Director
would have to say to You?⇨⇨⇨⇨

Did you get a pat on the back from the PR Director?

Or did the PR Director have a complaint for you?

OR did the PR Director say, "We need to go shopping at Nordstrom's and leave the Financial Director *at home!*"

The trend towards "Casual Day" in many office environments has left the Internal PR Director dazed and confused. It used to be very defined, now things are fuzzy but the Internal PR Director will not let down their guard. They still have a mission—to keep you looking "hip, slick and cool" all the time—and just because the goal posts have been moved doesn't mean the PR Director will be casual about it.

Did your PR Director suggest that you give more attention to this segment of your life?

Be aware that you may have an Internal PR Director whose mission is counterculture—that you aren't well presented unless you're shocking people a little bit with your taste. The directive of your PR may possibly be: anything but "normal" (whatever that is). This can be a tall order since we have such a wide latitude of styles nowadays. It can be exhausting to give an Internal PR Director this much work. If your dress criteria is "Is it weird enough?" this constant challenge can be creating stress. It takes a lot of effort (and sometimes a lot of money) to be perpetually counterculture.

Or are you locked into a certain color or colors? This is you and nothing else will do? To be seen in yellow, for instance, for you, would be to be "out of uniform." These restrictions can box a PR Director in. When corralled tightly enough, the Internal PR Director can put undue stress on the Financial Director. "I *must* have that black nail polish." "I *must* have these $220 athletic shoes." "I must." "I must."

A lot of people are at war with themselves inside. They think they want something but there's a part of them that has a higher need. They think they want to be out there in the world but there's a part of them that's holding them back. They think they can be thinner but there's a very powerful fat person inside. They think they want to get things done but they somehow get only 10 hours a day when everyone else gets 24. You can't get yourself to follow through on your best choices until you learn how to address the need in you that holds you back.

If you're sabotaging something—your marketing efforts, your education, your weight, your finances or your relationships—that means: some part of you wants it and some part of you doesn't want it.

It took a 15 minute negotiation to solve my lifetime weight problem. Statistically this problem has a 95% failure rate. My chances of succeeding were less than if I'd had a heroin addiction. And in 15 minutes I met, made contact with and negotiated with the inner part of me that had kept me fat my entire life. Sure I had overweight parents and brothers and aunts and uncles and nieces and cousins. They were all fat.

"Heredity is not destiny."
—T. Duncan

There are plenty of children of fat people who are not fat. There are plenty of children of people with other kinds of issues that don't have the problems themselves. Not all children of poor people stay poor. Your circumstances are one thing, your choices are another.

"Success is not a secret, it's a system."
—Alyce Cornyn-Selby

And now you can take the system that has been *using you* and you can turn around and *use it!*

This Inner Theatre system is a tool for people who no longer want to be unhappy in their lives and want to achieve real results and realize their goals. Remember: If you're fat and you're happy being fat then being thin *is not one of your goals.* I'm not here to give you a goal. I'm here to help you achieve the goals you have for yourself. The goal picking is all up to you.

For me it has been about Freedom. I have a high regard for this word. Before I understood this Inner Theatre method, I was frustrated because of what I saw as a lack of freedom. I felt that I should have the freedom to pick a number and make it happen. I should be able to pick a number on the scales and then weigh that. I should be able to pick a financial number and then make that happen. I should be able to pick a number as a deadline and meet that date. I should be able to pick a perform-ance goal of so many miles, so many minutes, so many blood pressure points and through effort, make them all happen. Being able to do this, to me, meant freedom. Not being able to do this meant that I wasn't free.

I was free to pick a goal, why wasn't I free to make it happen? I could be successful at some things but not others. I never missed a deadline at work but I could never hit the mark on the bathroom scales. I could succeed with a blood pressure measurement but I couldn't succeed with my savings account.

It is so frustrating to tell yourself that "this time" you're going to make it happen. This budget will work or this diet will work or this exercise program will work. Today is going to be different. Evening arrives and once again you've blown it. How is that possible? How could anybody want to hit that goal so much and then miss the mark?

It was a mystery to me. And I came to the realization that I could not trust myself. I could not trust myself with my own goals. I could not trust myself to do what I said I wanted done. That was a crushing day. I couldn't trust myself in buffet lines, in bakeries, in fast food places. When you can't trust yourself, you find yourself (logically) not trusting other people either.

I truly believe that there are people who are happy being fat and they really are beautiful being fat. I believe that there are earnest people who don't require a lot of money and really don't want to own anything.

I am not one of those people. I have a healthy, long list of wants for myself. I want to see me brush my teeth every day. I want to see me eat appropriately. I want to see me wearing a seat belt. I want to see me having quantities of money so that I can have the luxury of giving some of it away. I want to be able to find a British phone booth and drag it home and put it in my living room just for fun. I want to see the numbers go up on my investments. I want pleasant relationships and pleasant solitudes. I want to be a size 8 because then I can wear a size 8 or 10 or 12 or 18 or 24. But if I'm a size 24 I can only wear size 24.

I want to be able to pick a number and weigh it. I want to be able to pick a number and spend it or save it. I want to honor my agreements with myself. I want to be able to say, "I'm going to be sugar free today" and then actually do that. I want the freedom to say I'm going to do something and at the end of the day, say "OK, you did what you said you were going to do."

That's all. Just the freedom to be on my own page, to show up for my own parade. Is this too much to ask?

**"Why should we be angry that we cannot
make others as we wish them to be—
since we cannot make *ourselves*
as we wish to be."**
—Japanese proverb

It seemed to me that this simple striving for freedom was reasonable. I didn't think I was making unreasonable demands on myself. Yet there I was knowing what I was supposed to do and then not doing it.

It blew neurons in my mind to think that there was a part of me that didn't want what I said I wanted. I intensely wanted to lose weight. I thought that every fiber of my being craved a thinner Alyce. Well, how wrong could I be?

In 15 minutes I met the internal part in me that had a higher need and had her own Very Good Reason for blanketing me with 100 extra pounds. I met a winner. Obviously. She was winning and I wasn't. The weight was there and all my so-called "willpower" didn't stand a chance against her. I was being out-maneuvered daily by an internal part who felt that the best way for me to survive life on Planet Earth was to have an extra 100 pounds on, not off. And every day I bucked her and every day she won. She had the "higher need."

This internal part of me, in my case, was a female character but you may have a male counterpart or a ball of light or a pile of cloth. Your internal parts can show themselves in a variety of guises. Just let it happen.

When I asked you to listen to 3 different internal directors, that exercise should have taken you about 21 seconds, 7 seconds for each director. During those 21 seconds you received a lot of information. Some of your directors have been wanting to talk to you for a long time—to talk *uninterrupted* without the others jumping in. When I directed you to call them out singly, there was a reason for that. You need to give them center stage to let them speak without conflict just as the example with Jane. You heard the characters individually instead of as a chorus.

In a good, well-rehearsed choir you shouldn't be able to pick out individual voices, do you realize that? If they are a good choir, they sing as one voice. Individually they will pronounce the syllables differently so as to blend well together and the whole is heard as one. Choir singing is a beautiful act of teamwork. The difference between a good choir and the voices inside your head is: the choir has agreed to sing the same song at the same time.

What about the choir inside your head? Frequently the parts step on each other so well and they're *so fast* that you can't discern the individual voices. The Inner Theatre method slows things down. You don't want a chorus. You want to be able to hear the individual voices. Once you begin to hear them as individual value systems in conflict then you can begin to honor them. You can find the one with the "higher need." And once honored and listened to, then you can begin to negotiate.

So what does a negotiation look like?

It looks like a script. The following example is what takes place when a couch potato encounters a piece of exercise equipment on sale. Fortunately this person has the Inner Theatre method down and can hear the conflict between four different voices:

Health Director *(HD)*, responsible for issues of the physical body

Financial Director *(FD)*, responsible for fiscal issues

Space Director *(SD)*, responsible for home, hearth, environment

Inner Kid *(Kid)*, responsible for play and whining

For every you reading this there is also a You. You are the Manager of this Inner Theatre. You have the power to ask parts to report to you. You have the power to listen. You have the power to stop the discussion. You have the power to negotiate a strategy. This is demonstrated by the following person who has good self-management skills.

The issue: a specialized and expensive piece of exercise equipment is on sale and here is the conversation…

HD: Hey, this'll be great! Exercise! I'll finally get myself to exercise! I can exercise when it's raining, exercise watching TV…

FD: I don't know. It's still pretty expensive even on sale.

SD: Where are you going to put it?

Kid: In front of the TV! Exercise is boring, that's why I never do it.

SD: Oh, no, you don't! We've got a basement full of stuff like this! What about that trampoline?

FD: The Space Director's right! This is a lot of money to spend on something we don't know we're actually going to use…

HD: But I need it! If I had it I could get serious about getting fit! It's aerobic! It's easy on the joints! Look, it exercises upper body too!

SD: No! Absolutely not. We're not putting this thing in my nicely decorated bedroom. Just run around the block if you want some exercise!

Kid: There's bad guys out there…I don't want to run around the block when there's bad guys out there. And I'm not gettin' up at 5 A.M. either. I just want to watch TV.

HD: I'll feel better. I'll lose weight. Life will be wonderful! If I just have this machine, I'll make it happen this time. Let's get it!

FD: Well, it's cheaper than joining a health club.

SD: If this is another one of the things we get and don't use…NO! I can just see it collecting dust in the basement.

HD: I'll use it! I'll use it! What about cardiovascular health! Think of the benefits! Look at this newest article about heart disease!

SD: You'll end up hanging pajamas off of it in the bedroom! Think of the space!

FD: Think of the money!

Kid: Think I need a nap…

YOU: Hold it, hold it. Maybe we're finally ready to get motivated about exercising and maybe this *will* work. This thing is on sale for two weeks. What would it take to have everybody agree on a decision?

FD: Well, if it were free, I'd vote for it.

SD: If it folded up into the wall, I'd vote for it.

YOU: Seriously, would you be willing to support getting it if…

SD: There was a demonstrated effort about exercising, if I thought this was going to be a serious thing.

FD: Yeah, I could get behind it financially if I thought it wouldn't be a waste of money.

YOU: OK, what would demonstrate that?

SD: The price is good for 2 weeks. If I see us walk 2 miles every day for 2 weeks, then I'll know that we're finally serious about exercising.

Kid: How about 1 week and 1 mile...

SD: No!

HD: How about 2 miles 10 times in 2 weeks...

FD: Yeah, I'd like a few days just to have time to pay bills.

YOU: OK, the proposal before us is: if we walk 2 miles 10 times in the next 2 weeks, we'll order the machine. If we don't, we'll forget it.

Kid: And go play on the jungle gym at the park instead.

SD: At least the play equipment stays in the park! OK, agreed.

HD: YES!

FD: Oh, all right. But buy it out right; don't pay the finance charge. Maybe I can watch the stock reports on TV while we're using this infernal machine...

HD: (*wagging a finger at the Inner Kid*) And no greasy French fries for lunch today! And take your vitamins!

Kid: Don't push your luck...you *need* me!

An agreement is reached. A behavior is agreed upon. A demonstration must be completed and then a purchase can be made.

Notice that at *no time* did You attempt to talk any of the parts out of their opinions. None of the voices said, "You're an idiot! You shouldn't feel that way!" or "That's ridiculous!" This is the hallmark of a good self-management system. All parts are respected and all parts are heard. No matter how uncomfortable their ideas or "unreasonable" they appear, all parts are welcome. If they are ridiculed or chastised, they will go underground and they will sabotage the effort. Their messages will be shown to you in the form of a behavior "code." ***Your job is to*** *crack this code.* You do this by honoring, listening and respecting every part of You.

Everything I write, everything I research, everything I teach has one intent: to help you get what you want. The only problem is: you may not know what that is. You may think you want to have money but there's a part of you that has a higher need. You may think you want to have great health but a part of you has a higher need. You may think you want a lasting relationship but a part of you has a higher need for something different.

So what's your sabotage? In the chapters ahead you will find solutions for the Financial Sabotage, Time Sabotage (procrastination), Weight Sabotage and and Couples (relationship) Sabotage.

Important Note: The Inner Theatre is not a democracy. Depending on the issue, some parts will have more power than others. This complicates things slightly. It means that you can't just simply take a vote and have a decision. For instance, you may have an internal Financial Director that seems to be Godzilla, saying "no" to everything. Let's say you have no dental insurance and you have a toothache. Your monster-like Financial Director can keep you from getting help *for awhile,* hoping the problem will fix itself, but when the pain gets too intense eventually you will say, "I don't care! Take my IRA's! Just stop the pain!"

Are you a good guardian for all your internal parts?

When you get to know the parts of yourself you will find that communicating with these "characters" is more fascinating than a Shakespearean drama. It won't be frustrating any more; it will be entertaining. Once you have these internal parts working together you become very effective. Your behavior becomes cohesive with what you say you want. You're not "scattered" anymore; you're centered.

3 Ways of Getting in Touch with Your Internal Directors

Way 1: HAVE A DIALOGUE IN YOUR MIND.

Set aside a few minutes of quiet time, uninterrupted time. Your mind works very fast so not much time is required.

Close your eyes. Imagine the inside of a theatre. Picture the color of the walls, the fabric of the seats, the size of the stage, the type of floor covering and any details. See the stage and the comfortable chair that is your chair in the center of the stage. Sit in the center stage chair and look out across the theatre. Imagine that your parts, your internal directors occupy the theatre seats.

Ask to speak to the part in charge of whatever issue you would like to discuss.

When this part acknowledges, thank them. Ask them if they would be willing to communicate with you about the issue. When they say "yes," thank them. Be respectful, courteous, understanding and approachable.

Frequently other parts will join in the conversation and you will have to mediate. If the issue you are working on is a sabotage issue, then clearly it is because "part of you wants one thing and part of you wants something else." There is a portion of you that has a goal and there is another portion that has a higher need. This "higher need part" is most likely unknown to you and "speaks" to you through behavioral sabotage. So the message is delivered to you in code, remember.

Way 2: HAVE SOMEONE ELSE DIRECT A DIALOGUE.

Go to a trusted friend, counselor or therapist. Explain the concept of the Inner Theatre and have them walk you through a negotiation. Have them help you "make a deal" or "strike a settlement" regarding your future behavior. Set dates.

Way 3: HAVE A WRITTEN DIALOGUE.

With a yellow legal pad, spiral notebook, blank journal or your word processor (whether that's an antique known as a typewriter or a high speed laptop), write.

If you're hung up about getting started, begin by writing what you heard from your three internal parts from earlier in this chapter. You received a lot of information in 21 seconds (the average time on that exercise). To "prime the pump" and get things started just write down what you heard in that simple exercise when you met your Financial Director, Health Director and PR Director.

When you hear from a part that is new to you it is not necessary to I.D. it or give it a name. Call it "X" if you have to or "Mystery Guest" or any creative name. Just keep the flow going. The important thing is: they're talking and you're listening.

When you write, your inner theatre work will look like scripts as has been illustrated.

2 Possible "writing hang ups":

a) You have an internal perfectionist part who wants all sentence structure to have a verb and a subject. You pay attention to paragraph breaks when you write and you will stop your process to look up the correct spelling of a word. Do not do this. Tell your internal perfect writer person (the name of your former English teacher perhaps?) to take a much needed vacation while you do your Inner Theatre work. The important thing is *content,* pure, uninterrupted content and we could care less about punctuation and grammar. The purpose of this exercise is not how well you can edit yourself—in fact, it is just the opposite. So tell your internal Editor to go sit in the corner with a copy of the *New York Times* and try to find typos while you go about your more important work.

> **"Perfectionism is the voice of the oppressor,
> the enemy of the people.
> It will keep you cramped and insane
> your whole life."**
> —Anne Lamott

b) You had a teacher who punished students by giving them writing assignments. Hopefully this is a dying practice, but you never know. If you were ever told to "write that on the board 100 times" or to make up lost points you now have to write an essay, then chances are you still regard writing anything more than your name as a form of punishment. Let's change your perspective on that one.

Your pen (or your word processor) is now your **microphone.** When you are watching a television talk show, the host has a cordless microphone, usually one with a fuzzy foam cap on it. They use this "talking stick" by talking into it and you at home can hear them. When this person wanders out into the audience he or she extends the microphone to whomever they want to have speak. This audience person frequently leans toward the show's host and speaks into the microphone. Now you at home can also hear this person. When the host pulls the microphone away or tilts it back to their own mouth, your communication with the audience participant is cut off. Most of these television microphones are so directional that once they are two inches or more away a participant could scream additional information and it won't be picked up. This gives the host great control.

When you put a pen in your hand or when you type "F.D." into your computer, this is like putting a microphone up to the face of your internal Financial Director. This is the cue that they are now "on" and they have the floor. They can now be heard. Now they can speak to you right through your pen. Your pen is no longer a utensil for making ink marks, your pen has become a connecting rod between You and what's in You. It is now a microphone for your parts to communicate to You.

For you internet buffs, imagine that you are in your very own chat room and all the people who have logged on are part of You. They have identifiers so that you can understand the running commentary. This isn't the Internet—it's the *INTRANET* and you can receive much more important information (and information that is directly relevant to your own life) here than from any search engine on the World Wide Web.

NOW ALL THE PEOPLE WHO ARE REALLY RUNNING YOUR LIFE CAN TALK TO YOU—NOT THE PEOPLE *OUTSIDE* OF YOU BUT ALL THE PEOPLE ON THE *INSIDE* OF YOU.

The Security Issue: Usually what you write may be something that you would like to keep secret. When confidentiality is an issue, take steps to insure your privacy. The most trustworthy spouse will have difficulty keeping their hands and eyes out of your journal. Solve this problem before you begin, otherwise it will affect the quality of the intimacy between You and your parts. You will hedge, you will suppress their voices to have things be pleasant. Bad call. More than one relationship has ended when a partner's journal was read. And this may be the result of sabotage too. If you do not feel perfectly safe writing what you hear, think or feel no matter how embarrassing or painful it may be, then you probably won't be able to work on major issues.

You do not have to keep the dialogues that you write. The purpose of writing is to *process your issue.* The writing is recording the minutes of the meeting with your internal parts. You do not have to keep this record. Writing enables you to give undivided attention to the work and to negotiating.

Writing has the added advantage of keeping you on task. This is true for business meetings, why should it be any different inside your mind? When you attend a meeting and the leader keeps track of everyone's input by writing things on a board or flip chart, it keeps the meeting participants "on the same page." There is less side conversation, less deviation from the subject when everyone can see the writing. You can also keep track of where you are with a written agenda. Writing focuses the group. Well, writing focuses your inner group as well. Without writing, your dialogue may splinter and wander exactly the way it does in a poorly run company meeting.

Without the use of writing, your internal Duty Officer may overpower your other parts. You know what I mean when I say "Duty Officer." The one who reminds you to take the cat to the vet, have the oil changed in the car, take out the garbage, in short, the internal part who gives you your to-do list every morning. You may not actually get around to doing any of these things but you've got a person in there constantly telling you to do them anyway. Writing helps deflect the influences of this task master.

WRITE OFF YOUR ILLS

In one study, subjects were asked to spend 20 minutes writing intimately to themselves. When researches examined blood samples taken after the fourth day, they found evidence of an "enhance immune response." The trend continued for the following for six weeks. Participants who showed the greatest improvements in health were those who wrote about events in their lives! The act of writing can even show up in your blood stream!

If this isn't enough to motivate you to start writing to yourself, then consider this writer:

"I can shake off everything if I write;
my sorrows disappear,
my courage is reborn."
—Anne Frank

Your life may seem like a horror to you but it will not be the excruciating situation that Anne Frank endured. Reread the above sentence! "My sorrows disappear, my courage is reborn(!)" Then next time you think you need some courage in your life, the person you need to speak to is You.

Actress Sally Field has been an avid journal keeper since her mid-20's. Each time she finishes a journal, she forgets about it. "I never read the old ones," she says.

Actor Nicholas Cage keeps two journals. "I like to write in a journal," he says, "but sometimes it comes out angry. So I decided to have a dark and a light journal. I exorcise demons in the dark journal."

When you establish contact with your own inner directors you will be meeting some of the most fascinating characters that you will ever meet. Other forms of entertainment will pale by comparison. And this activity is interactive; you get to talk with these characters!

You'll never be alone again either.

And you can take your Inner Theatre and your Cast of Characters everywhere with you. Say, for instance, when you buy a car. Maybe the last time you bought a car, it was your P.R. Director's choice of a car. And this time you'd prefer that the Financial Director came along. Or maybe you're house-hunting and you would like to make a clear-headed decision about such an important purchase. You would appreciate it if your Internal Mom would be less vocal when you tour houses, otherwise you'll end up with a house only your mother would love. Case in point: a man designed and built his own house, did most of the construction himself. It wasn't until he was looking at the small scale model of the house that he realized where he'd received his inspiration. The little model was an exact replica of the bird house where his father kept his prized live birds. This father was one of those old-style dads who didn't show affection for family members and it seemed, to his son, that the only thing he truly loved was his birds. Fortunately the design functioned well as a house and so far as I know, is still occupied by the fellow and his family. Perhaps this was the "shape" of what he saw love as being and by creating that shape he really did have a place to put all the love that he needed inside of it.

When you honor and respect the parts of yourself, you will establish rapport. Eventually You become confidants with your selves and then, of course, be able to persuade. *You'll be in a position to influence yourself.*

The Chinese character for "learning" is expressed in two symbols, not one. One symbol means "study" and the other means "practicing constantly." Today we studied. Practicing is up to you.

> **"Having failed to conquer myself,**
> **my best hope now is to arrange**
> **an alliance with myself."**
> —Ashleigh Brilliant
> copyright Ashleigh Brilliant
> www.AshleighBrilliant.com

Actor Tim Allen says, "I'm constantly having dialogues with myself. It saves me countless hours in a therapist's chair."

And from comedian Jackie Mason: "I talk to myself because I like dealing with a better class of people."

What issue is important to you?
Who do you need to talk to right now?
Issue: _____
Internal Part: _____

5 Questions for a Desired State:
1. What do you want?

_____

_____

2. How will you know when you have it?
(What will it look like? sound like?)

_____

_____

3. How will having it affect your life?

_____

_____

4. What are you pretending not to know?

_____

_____

5. What's the worst that could happen if you:
a. get it?

_____

_____

b. don't get it?

_____

_____

Exercise

(This will be the single most important thing you do this year.)

Your sabotage:
  1. If you could throw the switch on it today, what is it? (The Weight Sabotage? The Financial Sabotage? What?)

_____

_____

  2. How would your life be different without it?

_____

_____

Chapter 6
Perfectionists and
Embarrassment

**"Perfectionism is self-abuse
of the highest order."**
—Anne Wilson Schaef

Perfectionists harbor 5 "irrational beliefs." They are:
    I must have control over all of my actions to feel safe.
    I must do everything perfectly or what I do is worthless.
    Everyone is aware of, and interested in, what I am doing.
    Everyone must love me and approve of what I do.
    External validation is crucial to me.

And, of course, I won't start until I can do it perfectly. I'll
have a party when the house is clean and the yard too. I'll buy
a bathing suit when I've lost 20 more pounds. I'll go to Europe
when I've learned enough Italian. I'll start a book when the kids
are gone.

Two distinctly different messages came out of my car radio
this morning. One was an ad that said, "Be all you can be." The
other was a song lyric, "Don't get above your raisin'." So which
is it?

"It is normal," writes career counselor Janet Cobb, "to live
with paradox: organized chaos, disciplined procrastination,
discouraged optimism and mediocre success. Ironically, as we
demand less perfection of ourselves, we find we can do more."

If you came from middle class overweight parents who
couldn't carry a tune in a bucket and you're *not* supposed to "get
above your raisin'," then chances are you'll sabotage any efforts
to be rich, thin or sing. At the same time, you'll feel guilty for not
"honoring your talents" and "going for the gold" and all the rest
of that rah-rah inspirational stuff. Your outward behavior will

resemble a car with an acceleration problem: you'll speed up, then hang back, then charge forward and then fall back. You'll pursue your dreams then have a "reality check."

Procrastination is a great way to handle this dilemma. Procrastination allows us to believe that our ability is greater than our performance. If we put off projects and then slam dunk them at the last minute, we can always coddle ourselves into believing that what we "could have done" would have been great.

> **"Nothing would be done at all**
> **if a person waited til they could do it**
> **so well that no one would find fault with it."**
> —unknown

I have watched people get over their perfectionism with the use of a simple white shoelace. They tie it in a bow around the handle on their desk drawer or around the handset of their telephone. The tied shoelace is a message that says: "You didn't tie it perfectly the first time you tried. *Nobody ever has.* And now you do it without even thinking about it. Whatever you do today does not have to be done perfectly."

Career counselor Joe Dubay sees people who refuse to recognize or deal with a problematic trait. "I recall a doctor who had been relieved of three different positions in hospitals and clinics—he was very much a perfectionist," Dubay says. "And of course, the more he got in trouble, the more rigid he became in his perfectionism. He was projecting his perfectionism and being critical of others. So the deeper he got into things, the harder he pushed...the very trait that was sabotaging him."

If you have an internal part who is holding you to an impossible standard, you need to have a conversation with this person. In fact, move aside and I'll do it for you. OK, I'd like to talk to the part of you that insists that things are perfect before you can a) think about it b) begin or c) finish. Hello there, Director of Perfect. Thank you for being there and for all your years of heroic effort. You have served well and we wouldn't have made it this far if it hadn't been for you. You deserve a lot of credit for our success so far. I'd like to try something different, however, and I need your help. But I can't really move off dead center without your support. Would you be willing to experience some discomfort while I experiment with some new things? After all, every drop of high performance gasoline starts out as crude oil. I want your help in finding my "crude oil" so that we can distill it into something you could be proud of. Would you be willing to help me do it imperfectly at first and then help me perfect it? I appreciate the fact that you know quality performance when you see it. You'll be able to recognize my imperfect attempts and see that they are perfect attempts for my level. I promise that this support will not end up turning me into a slob or start me down a road of sloppy behavior. Now, can I have an amen from you?

Another concern held by perfectionists is that "if I do this perfectly, everyone will expect all my behavior to be perfect." I will have to keep excelling and outdoing myself.

Show up for your own parade. Don't you ever wonder what it would be like to give it your best shot? Even if it fails you'll feel good and clear about yourself. But if you fail and *you didn't give it your best shot,* you'll always have that niggling voice that says, "I could have been a contender."

On their way to The Big Success, winning entrepreneurs have an average of 3.2 failures. I discovered this when I did the research for *Why Winners Win.* Henry Ford went bankrupt his first year in the automobile industry. His second company also failed. His third one has done rather well.

Twenty seven publishers turned down a children's book that went on to sell six million copies for Dr. Seuss.

Jack Matson, Ph.D teaches a creativity course for the University of Houston that his students call "Failure 101." He gives students assignments to build things with popcicle sticks that no one would buy, so they build things like hot tubs for hamsters. But when students equated *failure with innovation instead of defeat, they felt free to try anything.* What a gift! And here I was wasting valuable time by thinking that failure was something to be avoided!

**"The way to succeed is to
double your failure rate."**
—Thomas J. Watson

I read recently that only 25% of products developed by 3M, Microsoft and Proctor & Gamble are successful. They're throwing a lot of ideas and resources up against the wall and 75% of it *isn't sticking.* I want my success rate to be higher than that but it certainly inspires me to get in the game and get up to bat! You know, of course, that the strike out king of all time was none other than Babe Ruth. Then there's Wayne Gretzky who says, "You miss 100% of the shots you don't take."

What would you be doing if you knew you couldn't fail? Why not do it anyway?

I'd rather have a junkyard full of projects and products that didn't work than to end my life regretting all the things I didn't try. A friend of mine created such notable non-profit projects as Doc Duncan's Worry Jar, Wish Biscuits, Fish Pun Sculpture and the Wand R. Lust Company. They were tiny enterprises that stayed tiny and she looks back on them fondly as if they're tiny funny children who preferred not to grow up. That's sort of a sweet thing, isn't it? In my mind they were all totally successful because she enjoyed every minute of creating them.

Not all your wild ideas may take off like Pet Rocks. So?

My old friend Arthur Lind created a Love Cube that was nothing more than a painted block of wood with a hole bored through it. Two people were to put their fingers in the holes and touch. This idea hit during the '60's and 10,000 blocks were sold at Macy's in New York City the *first day.*

I learned a lot from Arthur. He created a successful office equipment business and sold it to his employees when he was 51 years old. After that Arthur would get passionately involved in his pet projects and these ranged from making bizarre furniture to remodeling old churches. Nothing ever dampened Arthur's enthusiasm for his own creations. The average life of his intense interest was two and a half years. It was remarkable how he supported his endeavors with his energy and time. He was totally in love with everything he created. With his perspective it was virtually impossible for Arthur to fail since his goal was to do something interesting.

Arthur was 74 years old when he shelved his interest in stencils and began to make hats. Arthur challenged and delighted himself. He didn't know how to sew so he taught himself and when he died there were three sewing machines in his living room where he made hats for theatre companies. His memorial service was attended by friends and an amazing display of his creations. One eulogizing woman said, "Arthur was Arthur's best friend." Another person said, "Go to your homes and your studios and make something with your hands. And if anyone asks you what you're doing, just say that you're 'arthuring' because Arthur was a *verb*."

The amazing thing about Arthur was that whatever endeavor he fancied, he had the support of 100% of his inner characters. Arthur showed up for his own parade.

I suggest that you take up arthuring. Arthuring is pursuing an activity without hope or expectations, just for the thrill of the activity itself. Arthuring passes no judgments. Arthuring is a very happy way to live. Arthuring is getting on your own page, suiting up to play in your own game. Arthuring is not hung up on results. Arthuring is the purest kind of fun. Arthuring is something you need to experience at least once in your life.

After years of writing successful non-fiction books I became hounded by a story, a novel, that would not leave me alone. I tried to suppress it and finally one summer I said OK, I just want this thing out of my system. I want it down on paper so that I won't have to be bothered by it anymore. Nobody is going to read this silly story, I said to myself but it has been bugging me for so long, I don't care anymore—I'm writing it.

**"Sometimes it's harder to kill a dream
than it is to make it come true."**
—Unknown

I gave up weeks and months of beautiful sunny weather to write *Did She Leave Me Any Money?* Two months after I finished writing it I had my first movie offer and it was optioned to Warner Bros. a month later. All of a sudden everybody wanted to read it. And I only wrote it because it was harder *not write it*.

Perfection? I love it when things are perfect. I wish everybody and everything was perfect. The cover of *Did She Leave Me Any Money?* had a typographical error. I don't recall ever losing any sleep over that typo.

Give yourself an assignment to: DO IT IMPERFECTLY. If you are river rafting for the first time and you hit the white water rapids, do you really care about form? No! You just care about getting through it without drowning! The next time you go through that set of rapids you may want to get through it without drowning *and* without flipping the raft. And the next time…

Would you lighten up on yourself? So what if you fail? Be honest—couldn't you handle it? It's how we handle failure that determines what we get out of life.

Some part of you has a burning desire to try something new and different. If you're not paying attention to that part, you're living a one-channel life. This part needs to voice itself to you…and you need to listen to it *and* to all opposing voices as well. Get your pen out and get all their opinions on paper. Write what your personal passion is…then write down all the reasons why this idea will never fly. Then write down how you're going to do it anyway. Negotiate a settlement. Pick a start date. Today you could do *some one small* thing that starts your project: buy a map, clip an ad, get paper, interview someone who has done it.

Your project could be anything from a Caribbean cruise to opening your own store. Remember if anyone asks you what you're doing, you can always say that you're arthuring.

Do something and something else will happen.

Dr. Dean Ornish has an interesting take on motivation. He understands that health information alone won't motivate people to change. He starts with patients who can't walk across a room without chest pain and he offers them surgery or a lifestyle change. On his program of learning better eating habits they are soon walking a mile pain-free. Even with this dramatic change, when they go home they don't always stick to the program. Since no one else was eating low-fat, low-cholesterol food, they begin to feel like freaks. Their pain comes back, but the pain of isolation is worse than the pain of the illness.

This is what I mean when I say "higher need." These patients have one need to be healthy and pain-free but they end up serving their higher need which is to be connected to others.

"We are all social creatures," Ornish says, "and ultimately what we want as much as being healthy is to feel we are connected with other people."

Anything that separates us from others then, no matter how rational or how good a choice it is for us, we may sabotage.

Well, this is pretty disgusting. Just because everybody else is eating donuts, that means you have to eat those fat pills too? If you are locked into being counterculture because all your friends are, do you really have to pierce some body part?

Our intense desire "to be connected" (Ornish's phrase) is killing us. So I have a request for myself and for you too. It is a simple request of my Inner Theatre. It goes like this:

"I need to put up with the embarrassment and/or discomfort of my successful solutions."

"Being in a support group helps heal the loneliness and isolation so common in our culture. When we work at that level, we find that many people are able to make and maintain lifestyle choices that are life enhancing rather than self-destructive," says Ornish.

Once those heart patients decided they wanted to save themselves from surgery and they agreed to the lifestyle change, perhaps their doctor should ask: "Would you be willing to be regarded as a freak in order to get healthy? Would you be willing to feel isolated from family and friends at the dinner table just to heal your damaged heart muscle?"

And if the patient says, "no, I wouldn't be willing to do that" then the doctor can direct them to the nearest marble cutting business to have their gravestone designed.

But what if the heart patient says, "Doc, I am totally, 100% committed to getting healthy and I am willing to put up with the embarrassment and/or the discomfort of the successful solutions."

If your "parade" is to be healthy, then show up! Stop frustrating the doctors and stop kidding yourself with your partial efforts.

Taken to the extreme, this desire "to be connected" keeps some people in cults and keeps them going to churches that don't serve their best and healthiest interests. This desire "to be connected" is the cause of many walks down many wedding chapel aisles with disastrous results. This desire "to be connected" is why some family members keep mum about incest and abuse.

This desire "to be connected" is probably why we keep living rooms as storage areas for furniture instead of using the space for our hobbies and interests. This desire "to be connected" is probably why I have a certain circle of sociopolitical women friends who all stay unhappily overweight. This desire "to be connected" is what keeps grass as the chosen plant life in our yards when just about any other plant would serve us better. Heaven forbid we should instead plant something indigenous that doesn't require chemicals and cutting and watering. Do not plant grass and then complain that it turns brown or needs to be cut *again* this weekend! That makes no sense! Heaven forbid that we should do something so rational (and so eccentric) as have a yard with no grass.

"I've been absolutely terrified every moment
of my life and
I never let it keep me from doing
a single thing I wanted to do."
—Georgia O'Keeffe

At some point in time you need to make a decision about all this. You need to stop lying to yourself about your heart problems, your living room, your lawn and your success. (When you stop lying to yourself, a miracle happens: SUCCESS.) If you're not willing to put up with the embarrassment and/or the discomfort of a successful life, then stop reading books about how to get your successful act together. Go eat a muffin, smoke a cigarette, put a bullet in a pistol and shoot yourself in the foot.

Your circumstances are one thing, your choices are another. You can't get yourself to follow through on your best choices until you learn how to address the need in you that holds you back. According to Dr. Ornish a huge need in human beings is this desire to be connected. How is this influencing your choices today? What's your sabotage?

(See also Chapter 9, Procrastination—The Time Sabotage, section on the Perfectionist Procrastinator.)

**"I used to be a perfectionist but
I stopped 'cause I wasn't good enough at it."**
—bumper sticker

Chapter 7
The Weight Sabotage

"A waist is a terrible thing to mind."
—diet center graffiti

"Imagine a place where people greet each other with open arms and give cheerful compliments like, 'You look wonderful! You've put on weight!'" writes Ellen Goodman. Well, she says (summing up a report by Harvard medical psychiatrist Anne Becker), this was life in Fiji before 1995. "Going thin" was considered to be a sign of a social problem and something to worry about. Then television came to Fiji and with only one channel the skinny people in the box took over the minds and tummies of the Fat Paradise Lost. Within 38 months the fat person *grand monde* became the fat *persona non grata*. Eating disorders doubled, bulimia with high school girls increased five fold. "The big success story of Western culture," notes Goodman, "is our ability to export insecurity."

If you like your life like it is right now, don't change. Please. Do not mistake this chapter for a sermon on what you should weigh. I've been fat and I've been thin and I had the same number of brain cells and the same sense of humor while being both. People seem to forget that. The essence of the person, their spirit, their grit, their drive, their love of certain music—these things don't change. There is a backlash against thin and it's no wonder since 70% of Americans think they're overweight and most of those people are just plain sick of hearing about it. Actress Nell Carter has expressed an uninhibited happiness about her size and about television's new big-think attitude. Another television actress Lesley Boone claims, "I've never let being overweight get in the way of anything I do."

If you're fat and you're happy being fat, be fat. If you want to be fat, then being thin isn't one of your goals. I am not here to give you a goal. I truly do not care what you weigh because whether I like you or not does not depend on your poundage. Perhaps because I came from the Fat World, I see people differently. The gift of my fat childhood is that I can usually see *people* instead of their packages. Their eyes and their voices tell me more of what I want to know. This transcends age, race, wheelchair and weight.

Think about it—what do all your friends have in common? Are they all the same age? the same weight? do they all earn about the same money? are they all gay? are they all straight? do they all come from your profession? or do you have the oddest array of mismatched people in your life? do you see "them" or their values? This is important to examine for two reasons:

a) the people you chose as friends says more about you than about them.

b) when you change (your weight or your finances, for instance) you may lose your "friends."

If you're a chi-chi black fashion style or Goth, how are your friends going to react if you show up in button-down Brooks Brothers? Is your *visual appearance* your ticket into how you are accepted by friends or family?

Do you have a friend who probably won't be a friend if you lose your weight? This is Fat Prejudice just as vibrant and provocative and loathsome as the employer who won't hire a fat person just because they're fat.

If you think there's no such thing as Fat Prejudice, then fasten your seat belt for this—three-quarters of young couples in a survey said they would choose abortion if told their fetus had a 50 percent chance of growing up to be obese.

Some research claims that there is a 95% failure rate for losing 20 pounds and keeping it off for two years. That makes it tougher (according to statistics) than kicking a hard drug habit. Only 80% of cocaine addicts fail. Your chances of overcoming obesity are less than overcoming cancer. With over 37 million Americans overweight, you're in good company. "Out of every 200 people who go on any weight-loss diet, approximately 190 fail," writes Bob Schwartz in *Diets Still Don't Work,* and of those ten who reach their goal, nine will gain their weight back within five years."

Well, if only 5% succeed, why not be one of the 5%? If only one person in the history of the world lost weight and kept it off that means there's a chance for the rest of us.

Because I have lost 100 pounds and kept it off, statistically speaking, I'm one in a million. And yet, I am not an extraordinary person—I'm an ordinary person who has learned an extraordinary system. (If you just checked into this chapter without reading the three chapters called "The Course," then you won't know what I'm talking about.)

I used to be fat. I didn't like it. My family didn't care if I was thin, in fact they preferred fat because they were all fat. But I personally didn't like it on me. I didn't like it any more than I'd like having to wear a chartreuse coat every day. I just didn't want to wear it anymore. I wasn't trying to lose weight to please anybody else or to get into a size 8 wedding dress or to measure up for an audition. There was no particular condition in my life that was pressuring me to take the weight off. There was no doctor who had issued a warning. But I was so heavy that when I lay down to go to sleep the poundage pressed against me making breathing difficult. I had 100 extra pounds evenly distributed over a nearly 5 foot eight frame.

"Inside there is a thin person
screaming to get out—
I ate her."
—T-shirt art

If you're fat and you'd like to weigh less, then we're on the same page. I think you should be able to pick whatever you want to weigh and then weigh that. This is the entire crux of self-sabotage: being able to call the shots and make it happen. This is not a social treatise on the merits of thin or the health problems of being fat. As far as I'm concerned it's your personal choice either way.

I never suggest that people lose weight because they'll lose the benefit of being overweight. Most people do a double take when they hear me say that. They have never once considered that there may be an advantage or a pay off for being overweight. I'm telling you that this is the start of solving your weight challenge if you just embrace this one concept.

If you rigidly react to the above paragraph by saying inside, "There is no benefit to being overweight!" then you are firmly entrenched in your belief system. This tells me that your internal fat person (the part of You that wants the weight on) is a winner, a gold-plated Olympic, Academy Award winning star. They have all the cards and You have nothing. Any attempt to lose weight will have a predictable outcome: You will gain it back and then some. Just to make sure. When you gain your weight back and you gain it all back *and then some,* this is a real indication that your internal fat person is in control and is teaching you a lesson. ***How about not ignoring the message this time?***

**"People don't get fat because they eat too much.
They get fat because they need to."**
—Louie Anderson in *Goodbye Jumbo*

Geraldo Rivera has done some unusual things on his television talk show but I watched one of his programs that really hit home. Geraldo was outfitted in a suit made of weights that had him resembling the Pillsbury dough boy. Latex was applied to his face and a make up artist did a masterful job creating the illusion of a 300 pound Geraldo. He had difficulty walking with his new weight and anchored himself in his audience. On stage his guests were people who had lost great amounts of weight and *gained it back.* Although Geraldo was obviously straining under the experience of being an obese man, one woman asked him how he felt. Geraldo answered, "Powerful. Like I could walk right through a wall." She said, "Exactly. And that's why I gained my weight back. Why do you think we have phrases like 'to throw your weight around'?"

It was an historic event for those of us who study self-sabotage. Here was a trim, fit talk show host experiencing what it felt like to be very, very overweight and even for the short time he did this, he recognized a benefit and he "got it on a cellular level." He wasn't told it second hand; he experienced it for himself. As uncomfortable as he was and *as uncomfortable as it is for those who have the excess weight,* the feeling of having the weight tells us that we can't be pushed over. There is an illusion of strength. He felt that he couldn't be blown off course. The panel of guests explained that *not* having the weight made them feel vulnerable and unprotected. For the first and only time on television, I felt like progress was being made towards actually understanding weight and why we might have it.

Not everyone has the extra weight on for reasons of power and stability but this program illustrated how different a person can feel with and without the weight. The guests were candid and provocative.

I took off the 100 pounds. Then I had to give myself what the weight had been giving me.

"Whose system did you use?" I get asked this all the time. I didn't use any commercial plan out there. Every plan will show you people who have been successful with their programs. I think they'll all probably work. But you have to work 'em. When they don't work, I'm assuming, it's because they were sabotaged, that is, their plans not followed.

I never tried the surgical route but I feel like I've tried everything else. Every goofy new diet fad found its way into my compulsive kitchen. The most provocative advertising must be those magazine ads for weight loss products because I still find myself reading them and itching to try their easy, eat-all-you-want new diet pill. Like Alice in Wonderland, a pill to make you smaller—what a delicious fantasy! If there is a weight-related news story on television, I stay glued to the set to find out what might be out there that will save us. A new synthetic fat, a chemical sweetener, an appetite suppressant that doesn't outright destroy you—anything! I'm fascinated by stories of people so overweight that they have to be lifted from their beds with cranes and taken to the hospital.

Author and researcher Anne Fletcher took a different approach when she wrote *Thin for Life.* She surveyed "masters at weight control"—people who have lost weight and kept it off. She quotes the diverse success plans of winners at weight loss. Somebody must be doing something right, Anne Fletcher figured, let's find those people and see what they're doing.

"I'm not saying that people should lose weight in this book, I'm just showing that you *can* lose weight," Fletcher said in *USA Today*. "I understand why many people have had it with the weight battle. And to a certain extent I applaud people who've accepted themselves heavier than the standard. But there is no way of getting around the fact that there are health risks of being overweight."

Anne Fletcher blows myths with her research:

Myth 1: If you've been overweight since childhood, it's next to impossible to lose weight and keep it off. Not true, say the masters interviewed. Most said they had been overweight since childhood.

Myth 2: It's impossible to lose weight once you've over 40. Not true. Most of the masters lost their weight after 40.

Myth 3: If you've dieted and failed many times before, there's little hope of ever solving your weight problem. Not true. Masters kept at it until they found a system that worked for *them*.

Myth 4: If you start regaining weight, you're bound to gain it all back. Not true. Masters were able to nip small weight gains before they got to be big gains.

You may have a genetic predisposition to being overweight. "It's genetic." That's a fact. But heredity need not be destiny. There are plenty of people whose parents are fat but they themselves are not fat. We can't change our genes, but we can change the way genes express themselves. We can change behavior. You can think of genes as if you're driving a car with wacky steering. You can override that steering. You may not like having to monitor your steering every day either. But genes are not commandments. We are, supposedly, the only animals on earth that can overrule our genes.

And we overrule our genes every time an alcoholic stays sober for 10 more minutes. We buck our genetics every time a shy person shakes the hand of a stranger. We beat the odds every day we stay away from sugar.

"Being loved by food had always been safer than being loved by people."
—Louie Anderson
in *Goodbye Jumbo*

"My mother overfed me as a baby," doesn't work if Mom is no longer cooking for you and you are no longer a baby.

A word about group support: choice. Many weight loss experts will flatly report that it isn't possible to lose weight without group support. Anne Fletcher's research says that group support is nice but not essential for all weight losers. Half the successful masters toughed it out alone. This is one of those areas where you really need to "know thyself." Some of us have the personality make up of long distance runners. We're best left alone in our own personal battles. Other of us are adrift without the anchor of knowing that there are other people out there with the same problem and a phone call from them is a lifeline.

"Food was often my friend, my comfort," writes a popular television reporter. "When I was good, I got a cookie. When I was bad, I didn't. Food became a reward, something connected to good behavior. I've been fighting that early conditioning for most of my life. Sometimes I'm more successful than other times, but oh, do I wish I could go back and reinvent the place food would have in my life."

"It's never about the food."
—Oprah Winfrey

TV's *Night Court* bailiff, Marsha Warfield was urged by viewers not to diet. "I got a lot of letters from women who felt Oprah had let them down and somehow invalidated them when she lost all that weight," says Warfield. "People write me saying, 'Please don't do that. You'll betray us.'" What nonsense! What gives some viewer the right to say such an outrageous thing!

And yet, this is insightful because you may be on the receiving end of such thoughts, even if your friends and family don't actually come right out and say it. Remember, our desire to stay connected with other people is one of the most powerful urges we have (see Dean Ornish's material quoted in Chapter 6).

Losing weight is an act of aggression.

It must be! Rarely do you find an overweight person who goes looking for conflict. Instead, they please their employers, their spouses, customers and children. And rarely please themselves. Pushy waiters, insensitive friends, sabotaging husbands and wives, unthinking parents make losing weight a chore. But when you've finally *had* it—when the fat hits the fire—you decide you want this for yourself. You want to pick a weight and then weigh that.

Anger is a great motivator when it comes to losing weight. In fact, I don't know how you can take the weight off and *keep it off* without it. Losing weight, in our society, is an act of aggression because refusing to eat and eat plenty is a symbol of rebellion. Hunger strike. Turning down food is turning down love.

It seems that the world is out to fill your face. Every holiday has with it a corresponding food. Hot dogs on the Fourth of July, Christmas cookies, chocolate Easter eggs, Halloween candy, wedding cake, Thanksgiving turkey, Valentine chocolates. If you don't participate in eating, you don't participate in the holiday.

It takes an aggressive person to say "no" to all of this.

There are friends and co-workers who will say, "Oh, go ahead. Just one donut won't hurt you. I brought them special just for you."

There is plenty to be angry about when in comes to weight.

Women's magazines! Somehow you are supposed to do all the exercises on page 34, bake the cake on page 35 and look like the model on page 36. It's a lie. It can't be done.

Restaurants! Armed with recipes designed to clog your arteries, the food service industry seems bent on slow homicide. Some restaurants feature "heart-safe" entrees. Yet there are whole boulevards of restaurants in this country with little to offer the person trying to get thinner and stay that way. Those of us working on weight issues find the good restaurants and limit our dining out to these few places.

Your spouse and family! "You've been so good on your diet, honey, let me take you out for ice cream." "Don't go on a diet! Every time you go on a diet you get grouchy!" "You don't need to lose weight, I like you just the way you are." "Here let me get my arms around those love handles." "The more of you there is, the more there is to love." Now, why in the world would your spouse try to sabotage your weight? Why, indeed? Because you're easier to control when you're fat. Because (they hope) nobody else will find you attractive. Because your spouse wants to be fat too. Because you're less active when you're fat.

A sampling of Thoughts to help you get the weight off and keep it off:

"I want this for myself."

"I can do this."

"I want the control."

"I have a right to be whatever size I want."

"No thyself."

"I have: energy enough, strength enough, discipline enough and guts enough."

"Nobody is going to look after me. It's nobody else's job. I will look after myself."

I didn't create the world of food the way that it is today. All I can create now is a battle plan for me to succeed. I no longer fight myself. Anger is energy in action. Can you get anger to work for you? Answer this next question: "Am I angry enough with this situation yet?" Because when you are angry enough you will do what needs to be done and you'll do it NOW. This is true for weight loss and everything else in your life too.

Successful weight loss is as much a mental challenge as a physical one.

The weight sabotage has two components. The physical component is food and exercise. At its simplest, when you consume more calories than you use, overweight is the result. Even today, it's pretty difficult for me to grasp this cause and effect. How is it that one six ounce piece of chocolate cake will materialize as two pounds of fat on me when I get on the scale? And I'm supposed to eat a box car full of lettuce instead?

OK, it makes little sense but that's the way it is. There is no getting around this and don't be taken in by the term "fat-free." Just read the calorie counts on those cookies! Yikes! They're loaded.

Read the labels. Study what's in the food and come up with your own list of what you can have plenty of, what you can have a little of and what you'd better stay away from. Unless you've just crawled out of a cave somewhere, you already know this information. If you don't, it is readily available. There's a library full of it at every grocery store check out counter. And none of it is new.

Be aware that there are "food triggers"—foods that for whatever reason, seem to set you off. Allergies have long been suspected of causing binges. I have listened to over 500 hours of compulsive overeaters share their stories and many people identified wheat as a food trigger. It takes trial and error to i.d. your food triggers—but each time you crash and burn is an opportunity to learn more about your complex physical urges. Another woman says "no thanks" to sugar free chocolate because "it sets me off."

GREAT PIECE OF ADVICE

Give it up for 6 months and see if you like your life any better. (That goes for food, shopping, relationships, you name it!) What a strange and wonderful and logical piece of advice! Why did it take more than 30 years for me to find it? My story: when I first heard this I decided to give up alcohol. Fortunately eliminating alcohol from my life was no big gut-wrenching ordeal but I learned two valuable lessons. No. 1: it was fully 6 months before I recognized the affect alcohol was having in my life and No. 2: there is freedom in deciding. I had it hardwired in my mind that eliminating something from life meant deprivation, the near opposite of freedom. What I learned, however, was that once I made the decision of no more alcohol, I didn't have to *redecide* every evening, shall I have a little wine with dinner or not? And shall I have one glass or is two OK? I simply became a person who doesn't drink alcohol period and that was the end of the discussion. When asked if I want to see the wine list I already know the answer. I don't have to think about it. It's a done issue. That, for me, was very freeing. Once I *got* this concept I was able to apply it to other things like donuts, exercise, people and even watching the news on television.

You may not realize this but every day you decide *not* to eat asphalt. Sounds a little crazy, doesn't it? But you know that you are a person who does not eat asphalt. You don't have to think about it. It's not an issue with you. I discovered what you may have known all along: eliminating things from my life was enhancing the quality, not restricting my freedom. I had more energy as a result because I wasn't constantly redeciding issues for myself.

I had a successful food strategy that lasted about 15 years and if I stuck to it, I was a fine weight. Then it failed me. Or was I failing it? Or was I being force fed by aliens in the middle of the night? I took an 8 week course offered by a local hospital and it confirmed that I was on the "right" track. I wrote down every bite of food I ate, just as I was instructed to do. By doing this I was able to see that I was *not sabotaging my efforts*. Still, I was the only one in the class who actually gained weight on this plan. How discouraging! Only momentarily, because it showed me that something was wrong—not with my motivation—but with the food. I made an adjustment in my food plan to accommodate my bouncing blood sugar and the extra weight came off again.

So on this food issue, I can't and won't give you a food plan. If you really are serious about losing weight then keep a list of everything you eat. Go over that list and identify what's wrong, what's not working. This is the one time that you need to be absolutely diligent. Do it for just a week. In fact, tell yourself to eat what you want but that once you eat it, you write it down. Just do that. At the end of the week, you'll have enough data to begin to coach yourself.

Day #: _____ **Date:** _____ **Day of Week:** _____

		Calories	Carbs	Sodium	Protein	Other
Breakfast	**Qty**					
_____	_____					
_____	_____					
_____	_____					
_____	**Totals**					
Lunch	**Qty**					
_____	_____					
_____	_____					
_____	_____					
_____	**Totals**					
Dinner	**Qty**					
_____	_____					
_____	_____					
_____	_____					
_____	**Totals**					
Snacks	**Qty**					
_____	_____					
_____	_____					
_____	_____					
_____	**Totals**					
Other (water, vitamins, exercise, meditation, etc.)						
_____	_____					
_____	_____					
_____	**Daily Totals**					

If you truly don't know what you, in all your uniqueness, are supposed to eat then get educated. Read. There are people reading this who think that "high cholesterol" is a Jewish holiday. In order to make good food choices, you need to know about food. You're smart; figure this out.

It is estimated that if the 37 million overweight Americans each took off 25 pounds, annual health care could be cut by $100 billion.

If you were going to go into a legal dispute in court, wouldn't you want to know everything about the opposition? What company doesn't want to know about their competition? If you're serious about losing weight, get to know the territory. If one strategy doesn't work (and you've followed it diligently) then switch to another strategy. **Stop doing what doesn't work.** If a high carbohydrate food plan isn't getting you results (and you've followed it to the letter) then try high protein for awhile. The only sure fire way to try out a food plan and not have sabotage in the equation is to write it all down.

My two favorite words used to be: Bakery Open. Now I know that there's only one reason for me to be in a bakery and that's to reminisce.

"If you don't want to slip, stay out of slippery places."
—Lynn Easton

You wouldn't expect a diabetic to eat your German Chocolate cake, would you? Then don't expect me to eat it either. You wouldn't be insulted if someone with an allergy to shellfish had to turn down your lobster bisque, would you? My desire to be a normal size is no less important to me than a diabetic's need to be sugarfree. Let's face facts. The most dangerous foods for our bodies are the foods that are decorated and dressed up the most: it's the stuff made with fat and sugar. I am not a diabetic but sometimes it is useful for me to regard myself as if I have a special medical condition that prevents me from eating certain foods. It makes staying away from those foods easier.

When I took a nutrition course offered by my corporate employer, the most knowledgeable person in the room was the student with the most amount of weight to lose. She knew *everything* about food and carried 125 extra pounds. And all this knowledge didn't help. That brings us to the next part.

The second component is mental. This is where I take a detour from standard approaches. Conventional "wisdom" says that if you feel good about yourself and love yourself enough you will take good care of yourself and not be overweight. The flip side of this has created the erroneous mind set: fat people have low self-esteem and must not like themselves. This absurd notion is an insult and it's also false. It does *not* require self-esteem to select an apple over apple strudel. All it takes is being smart about your choices and not sabotaging.

Do all thin people have great self-esteem? Know any thin people who don't love themselves?

"There has never been a link established between self-esteem and accomplishment."

This is the second time in this book I have given you this statement and I've done that because it flies in the face of convention and you need to really get this. I don't want to talk about self-esteem. I want to talk about accomplishment. Criminals typically rate higher on self-esteem tests than college students. If weight loss is the goal, you don't have to feel good, bad or indifferent about yourself. It'll make your life easier and probably more fun if you love yourself but it won't change the calorie count in any food. And it won't insure success at weight loss.

How about attitude? If you just have a great attitude, then everything will be fine, right? This approach may work for you but it doesn't work for me. I will readily and openly admit that I have a lousy attitude about food and this whole weight thing. If I had my way ice cream would be a vegetable. And it's not. I don't have to like the situation, I just have to take care of business.

I used to have myself believing that the free food samples they handed out at the grocery store were also free of calories. That's just another one of my personal lies to myself. I growl when I pick up a magazine and see a recipe for a high-fat, high-sugar pie on the same page as how to be as thin as a fashion model. It's infuriating to be expected to entertain people in your home with beautiful food, carry on intelligent conversations about the latest in restaurants and support every bake sale while wiggling willow-like in size 6 pants. I personally just can't do it.

"Looking back, my life seems like one long obstacle race, with me as its chief obstacle."
—Jack Paar

I cannot recommend my own strategy. It may be too bizarre for you. *You must do what works for you.* What works for me is generally regarded as eccentric. Back in the old days when I fixed dinner for my family, I would frequently serve the meal and then, if I felt my discipline wane, I'd go take a bath and sit in the tub until the good food smells were gone. Radical behavior? Sure! Did it work for me? Yes!

It is more important to me that I have things work in my life than to have things be conventional. I can't give you an exact date but at some point in time I had to stop kidding myself and say, "I'm not like everybody else and so everybody else's solutions don't work for me." I gave up. Being conventional went out the window but what came in was the freedom to find new things that did work for me.

I got rid of my oven. I donated it to a worthy cause. (You don't have to get rid of your oven; I'm just illustrating to you how unconventional some people get when success is important to them, in this case, me.) I had been very good at making homemade goodies and I was ready to dump that image of myself as master candy maker if it meant being successful at weight loss. I found a "Self-Service" sign from an old ARCO gas station and I posted that prominently in my kitchen. I took myself off the hostess track and now everybody knows that if you want something good to eat, you don't stop by Alyce's house.

When served food in a restaurant that I didn't expect and think I can't resist, I'll empty the pepper shaker on that food. Embarrassing to have to do this? Of course! Effective? Yes! When on an airplane, I pack my own food and eat that instead. It was only embarrassing the first ten or so times I did it.

Are you willing to be unconventional in order to take care of yourself and get what you want? Sometimes in life it comes down to that. I know of one woman who can cook like a dream and has complete self-confidence that she will not eat one bite of her own creations. She maintains a 70-pound weight loss and she bakes and donates elaborate desserts to fund raisers, has lavish dinners for people who "know food" and her husband is into gourmet cooking. I admire this woman. And this woman is not me. I will never be her.

I discovered that there are lots of ways to celebrate occasions that do not involve food but it takes a mighty creative person to do it. I stopped eating birthday cake, even if it was mine and even if my mother baked it (after repeated pleadings that I don't want sugar around me!). I worked and worked until I knew what I wanted on my food plan. And if it's not on the plan, it doesn't come into the house. I have little willpower. Admitting that you're not strong is very liberating. Taking steps to create an environment for someone who has a weakness for food (namely me) became a high priority.

> **"For a compulsive overeater certain convictions**
> **are the bitter enemies of truth.**
> **The conviction that if I had enough willpower I**
> **could overcome anything pushed me**
> **ever deeper into the mire of addiction."**
> —Overeaters Anonymous

What kind of environment would you create for a fat person who wanted to be thinner? Would you leave their kitchen cabinets full potato chips? Would you insist that they continue to bake holiday cookies? Would you expect them to join in the fun and pig out at every social function? Would you expect them to say "yes" to every Sunday buffet? Then get real, why do you expect it from yourself?

I discovered that taking the "stiff upper lip" approach to life (just buck up, girl!) usually brought me a fat lip (I'd get clobbered!). But if I said, "I'm a wuss and I'm fragile and I need special handling"—that approach worked for me. I learned that there was something endearing about asking for help too.

> **"Losing weight, I realized, is like removing a tattoo.**
> **It's going to hurt like hell.**
> **If I was finally going to be successful,**
> **I had to admit the pain."**
> —Louie Anderson
> in *Goodbye Jumbo*

So what got me started, what was the Turning Point? When I was at my heaviest the entire country was in social and political upheaval and I was not in control of Southeast Asia or who was sent there. I wasn't in control of which one of our nation's leaders was to be assassinated next. The country's collective psyche seemed to be at odds with itself, there was polarized opinions on everything. Nobody seemed to be in control. All problems seemed to be huge important problems and my weight just didn't seem to be something important enough when compared to everything else.

Finally it occurred to me that I was not in control of where I lived, when I'd be moving, what happened to my friends or what happened to the country. I was not in control. And this was not a temporary situation. I was never going to be in control of those things. I was powerless to stop warfare, hurricanes, traffic jams, telephone solicitors or any other kind of cancer. I was terribly racked by all this. And being terribly racked wasn't helping either.

I decided to control the only thing I knew I could control—what went into my mouth. I've never been anorexic but I've studied their interviews and they say pretty much the same thing. I heard the term "weight *control*" for the first time and it hit me like a thunderbolt. It hit me that I was *not* in control of some thing I actually *could* control. The word "control" became a mantra.

So I guess I'd have to say that the first thing a person needs to do to accomplish something that is statistically difficult is to **make it a priority.** Make it important enough in your mind to work on it. "Work on it" means you are willing to spend time, money and effort and do "whatever is necessary" to make this happen for you. You are going to put your resources, however meager they are, into this project. Have you just been dabbling at weight loss? Is it something you do more like a hobby—when you feel like it? Or are you a serious professional weight loser? Deciding to make it a priority will set up information out there to find you. When you hone in on the idea, the products and people you may need to help you succeed will somehow be drawn to you.

To be successful at weight loss **it can't be a hobby** with you. It can't be something you do only when you're feeling good or only when things are going well. It is a full time, every day, top-of-the-priority-list thing.

If you saw a toddler who was about to drink poison you would rush to get the bottle away from their lips, wouldn't you? Then why do you hesitate to push it away from your own?

There is one school of thought that says we should not think of any food as good or bad. That's a lovely sentiment and one that doesn't work particularly well for me. Perhaps it will work for you.

The answer to the Weight Sabotage is that there is a higher need inside You. Everyone that has the weight on has a higher need for the weight than they do for being thin. For some people that "higher need" is the overwhelming desire to be connected, as Dr. Dean Ornish suggests. To break bread together has such a universal appeal. In the old style religion "grounding" was needed after spiritual ritual and that involved the sharing of food.

The best place to listen to people talk about diets and losing weight is to eavesdrop in a restaurant or ice cream shop. The Weight Sabotage is one of the easiest to identify because we're actually wearing the results around our middles. It is fascinating to me to hear two people discussing the merits of Weight Loss Clinic versus Diet Center while polishing off two desserts a piece. (I watched this actually happen.) I encourage you to witness this phenomenon for yourself the next time you're out dining. Wherever people gather to eat you will hear conversations about cholesterol and fat and weight.

When you read The Course (Chapters 3, 4, 5) your internal person in charge of your weight also read those chapters with you.

Remember that these internal parts are your Survival Mechanisms. And that's what they are doing inside your mind. They all have different ideas about what constitutes your survival, however. And they can be difficult to listen to because they use words like: "should," "must," "have to," and "ought to." They are frequently demanding and unreasonable. Survival Mechanisms are rarely logical on the surface or at first glance. Once you understand their agenda, however, they are perfectly logical. They have their own ideas. And they are all vying for attention and air time in your mind.

Every day life is a series of compromises, whether you're buying vitamins or selecting a movie for this evening. Sometimes you like the compromise, but often something inside of you is left wanting. If this internal "wanting" goes on long enough and it is important enough, sabotage is the result.

Self-sabotage is when two or more internal directors are fighting each other. Part of you wants the weight off. If that part were unopposed, you'd be a perfect weight. But there is another part of you that wants the weight *on*.

We appear to be complex, inconsistent, often irrational, self-defeating and confused. We do not understand why we lose weight and gain it back. We start projects and never finish. We intend to do "good works' and never seem to get at it. In short, we are a mystery to ourselves.

What can be gained by a dialogue with your internal directors is understanding what motivates you. Instead of making no sense, you will begin to see that you make a lot of sense. Your directors, if allowed to speak to you, will tell you why you do what you do.

Self-sabotage is not always obvious. We may have sabotaged a job or a relationship and never knew that we were sabotaging.

But with weight, we know. Either we are the size we say we want to be or we aren't. And this is clearly self-sabotage because we are doing it to ourselves. It can be considered self-sabotage when we have clear options and we take the undesirable one repeatedly. When we say, "I want to *lose* ten pounds," and then we reach for the food that will *add* 10 pounds, that's sabotage.

The Nature of the Problem

Don't believe anyone who tries to tell you why you have your extra weight. You are the only one who knows—or more accurately the person who knows is inside you, not outside you.

For every person who has the extra weight, there is another reason to have it. This is a complex issue, but individually a simple one. So whatever the cause of your sabotage, it will be uniquely yours.

I have a different perspective about fat. I think that it is doing something for us. The task is to find out what.

This idea may be so new and so radical to you that you resist it as you read this. The idea the I should suggest that your extra weight has a benefit to you is, well, ridiculous. You may even begin to feel anger at the idea that what you have been trying to get rid of all these years is actually something that you'd need.

Just for a moment, pretend that you have your weight on for a Very Good Reason. Just pretend. If that reason were known to your friends, co-workers and relatives, they would all applaud you and say, "that's an excellent reason." No one would try to take your fat away and no one would suggest that you lose it, if they only knew this higher need.

If someone wants to lose weight and they aren't (and there's nothing medically wrong), it's obvious that someone on the inside wants the weight on. This person on the inside believes that having the weight on is a good idea. Their message to you is written in code. Your job now is to crack the code.

Finding the Very Good Reason

Imagine.

Get comfortable. Imagine the inside of a theatre. Have it your way: the Roman Coliseum, a movie theatre, a grandstand, bleachers at a ball game or a small intimate dinner theatre. This is yours; create what you want.

Conjure up the seating. Imagine the floor. Create the center stage. Imagine a very comfortable chair in the middle of center stage. Imagine You are in that chair. Look out over the audience. There are entities in the theatre seats. All of your good old friends are there: the Financial Director, the Health Director, your PR director, etc.

Say or write, "I want to speak to the person who is responsible for my weight."

(Do not ask to speak to the Health Director. If you are overweight, the internal person responsible for weight would *not* be the Health Director otherwise, you'd weigh your perfect weight.)

The tone of your conversation is respectful and cooperative. This is a negotiation. Continue your conversation.

Say or write: "Would the person responsible for my weight please stand up."

Thank them when they respond. (If you get no response, explain that you are willing to be approached at a future time and that you will honor whatever needs they have. Add: you want to continue the conversation. You may have to convince this inner part that you can be trusted. Work on another issue with another part.)

Next step. "Would you be willing to communicate with me about the issue of my weight?"

When this entity answers in the affirmative, say or write, "Thank you."

(Don't be surprised if you don't make contact on the first attempt. Remember you've been going against this part's efforts for a long time. I logged over 20 years of bucking the part of me that wanted the weight on. Also, this isn't AT&T, you may have to hang up and try again later. If you are ill or very tired or very frustrated, you may experience static on the line, sotospeak.)

You may want to ask:
    "Of what benefit are you to me?"
    "What is important to you?"
    "How can I help you?"
    "You have protected me all these years. I appreciate all that you have done for me. What do I need protection from?"
    "What is your purpose?"

Continue your conversation until it is appropriate to ask:
    "Would you be willing to work with me on this weight issue?"

And then,
    "Can I meet your need for _____ (whatever is needed) without the use of weight?"
    "How can I gain your support in my efforts to take off weight?"
    "Would you be willing to help me take off five pounds and then we can talk again?"
    "Is there some other way—any other way—you could be made comfortable without using excess weight as the means?"

You cannot simply rush through these questions. You must be willing to *do for yourself* what weight has been doing for this part of you.

For instance, if the issue of weight is connected to "assertiveness with the opposite sex," you are going to now be challenged to be assertive with the opposite sex instead of relying on the weight to do it for you.

Your Internal Fat Person wants a lot more than affirmations. Internal parts want strategy and action. It's not good enough to say, "OK, I'll feel protected starting right now." *You must do what ever it takes to feel as protected as the weight makes you feel!* What would make you feel safe? A full time body guard? (I am absolutely serious here.) Bullet proof vest? Pack heat? Take up a martial art? How about a good course in assertiveness—learning to communicate verbally the message "back off!" while still appearing to be a sweet person. Would that do it?

Next step. Pick a reachable goal weight—from 1 to 5 pounds. Pick a date. Get agreement.

Then ask, "Is there anyone else here who has an issue related to this weight loss and the new behavior?"

(It is likely that one or more additional characters or parts will voice an objection. Each part of You will have to be appeased before the successful negotiation is complete.)

Your internal PR Director, for instance may have a problem with exerting more assertiveness. This part may feel that relations at work will be strained if this new plan of behavior is allowed. Create successful scenes where you can see yourself being assertive and also being accepted in work situations. Try on strategies. Practice on the stage of your Inner Theatre. It's OK to try on a script and then rework it if You think it won't be easy enough for you to play. Be creative. If you get stuck for a solution to a sticky situation, ask yourself, what would _____ (pick a person) do in this situation?

When the negotiation is complete (and you will know it when you feel it) there is serenity that some people call "peace of mind." It comes from *pieces* of your mind joined together, thus *peace*. The weight comes off without white knuckling it because your inner winner, the person who has put the weight on, is now responsible for taking it off.

Keys to Making This Work

Do not attempt to bully or power trip in your Inner Theatre. Your directors may have some unreasonable, irrational and even amusing ideas about your survival. Don't try to change their opinions or tell them "not to feel that way." Instead, work with what you get. Accept whatever they share with you.

They are entitled to their opinions and it's not a good idea to try to change them or threaten them. You can negotiate.

What if your inner directors are stubborn and irrational?

Have you ever negotiated with someone who *wasn't* stubborn and irrational? No! If they were "rational" (according to your way of thinking) then they'd agree with you and you wouldn't be in a negotiation. Therefore you will never be in a "negotiation" with a rational person!

If it all made sense, you would have had the weight off a long time ago. But you're still fat and your Fat Director is still winning.

You know that it is unhealthy and uncomfortable to have the weight on...and you still have it on. Where has your logical, surface-level mind gotten you?

Your Fat Director is doing an excellent job and now you must deal with him/her. Other parts of You may object to your losing the weight too. It may put additional pressure on them to perform. Your Sexual Director may be threatened. If you have an internal part responsible for monogamy, they may be terrified. Your director in charge of Family Relationships may see problems ahead for you if you lose the weight. If everyone in your family is fat and you lose your weight, that is the same as telling them that they are wrong. If you've never stood up to family pressure before, this could be threatening.

You may have an internal part who is in charge of Historical Traumas. This entity keeps track of the awful moments in your life and remembers "what you weighed when." The Historical Trauma Director will try to keep you away from a certain number on the scales that may be associated with trouble. One woman explained that she was terrified to weigh 136 pounds. When she had hit this goal weight *twice* before she had been mugged while jogging. She continued her favorite form of exercise (running) and continued to lose but her anxiety protected her from getting within 10 pounds of her goal weight. Can't you be creative and think of solutions to her problem? Sure! Jog with a friend or buy a treadmill, trade services with a health club for the use of their indoor track—any number of possible solutions. Unless, of course, she likes being terrified.

People get what they want even when they don't realize it.

An agreement must be made in the Inner Theatre before a change in behavior will happen that is lasting. This can be accomplished with or without your conscious awareness.

Once you have asked for support and received agreement, turn the problem over to the biggest winner in your Inner Theatre. That will be the person who has been responsible for keeping the weight on. This part of you is a winner, right? Or you'd have solved this a long time ago.

Any good manager will tell you that *you give the most difficult task to the most effective person*. So give the task of taking the weight off to the person who has kept it *on*.

> **"I am a spy in the house of me.
> I report back from the front lines of the battle
> that is me."**
> —Carrie Fisher

Time is important to your Inner Theatre. When you make an agreement, set a time limit on it. Agree to reevaluate the situation in three months, for example. If the weight has come off and you are having problems, you may want to rethink your decision to lose the weight. The weight loss may have scared you because now you have proof that you can talk yourself into action. Any number of things can happen, so agree to check in and reevaluate your new situation.

What Others Learned When They Cracked Their Codes

Denny: "I had never had a weight problem before. I was a professional sports car driver for 15 years and I was having a good season. All of a sudden I gained weight and I was almost too fat for my fire suit. My fat was telling me to get out of driving and go back to managing the race team. My career was tied up in my weight. The weight was a protection reaction that I had following the crash and death of a racing friend."

Paul: "I feel a great deal of accomplishment when I run marathon races and I do well, very well, for someone who is over 40 and in a non-physical profession. The hours of training and running would take me away from my family and I felt guilty about this. Well, I get a back pain whenever I weigh 20 pounds more than I should and I won't run when my back hurts. My extra weight was just from the part of me that wanted to stay home with my family."

Susan: "My fat ruined a career for me in sales. I turned to designing and building furniture…something I really wanted to do in the first place. I started my own business. I kept the weight on to make sure that I'd never leave my business…I don't want to give myself the option of going back to working for anyone else. I prefer the solitude of my shop to the pressure of meeting people."

Kim: "I beat the big one—cancer. Although I was out of danger, I had 25 extra pounds on and I was disgusted with myself when I couldn't get it off. When I did this Inner Theatre technique, I remembered that all the people who were in chemotherapy with me were thin…and they all died. I was keeping the weight just in case the cancer came back and I would need it some day. I negotiated a 15 pound weight loss and I'm not going to fight with myself over the last 10."

Cheryl: "I'm a management consultant and I don't want to communicate 'cute' or 'pretty'; I want to communicate 'substance.' These extra 15 pounds are helping to anchor me so that I can't be thrown off base. I'm going to stop fighting with myself about the weight. I also read that women who are vice-presidential level and above average 25 pounds of extra weight."

Boker: "I knew my wife didn't like fat men so on every business trip I stayed away a little longer and came home a little fatter until finally she left. Now that I've lost 126 pounds, namely Sue, I imagine these 65 pounds will come right off."

Barb: "Twenty years ago I tried out for head cheerleader and I didn't make the squad. I put the weight on then and I've kept it on all these years as a form of rebellion. I have been rebelling against the Ideal Female look. I wanted (and still want) to be liked for who I am, not what I look like. My weight has remained as a kind of test to others. If people can't get past how I look, who needs them? I figured out that I can create other ways of testing the sincerity of people without using my weight to do it. I don't need this weight as a screening mechanism any more."

Patricia: "I was plump at my wedding and then gained 60 pounds. I was also very young when I married and I hadn't really had an opportunity to sow any wild oats. I discovered that the extra pounds were my way of keeping my distance from men. I didn't feel like I could trust myself and I wanted my marriage to work. I was using my weight to insure my monogamy. Having the weight on was my way of coping with men hitting on me. I discovered from this exercise that I need to develop skills at handling these tough situations instead of thinking the weight is going to make men leave me alone. It's not working. Since it's not working anyway, I might just as well lose it and be healthy."

Jeremy: "If you had a stick in front of you and a collie puppy in front of you, which one would you reach for first? Sure, the collie puppy. My survival mechanisms told me that if I wanted to get touched, I should look like the collie puppy. I have been built like a collie puppy most of my life because I wanted to be touched and now I'm ready to try something different. I got a lot of reinforcement as a child to look cuddly. That was OK for then but I've worn that act out. I'm ready for something different."

Allen: "I'd always been hefty and once in my life I was getting the scales to go down instead of up. I was swimming regularly and getting fit. One day I was in the pool and I was actually thinking about how much I weighed, imagining myself getting on the scales and seeing the number when suddenly my body cramped and I nearly drowned. During the shock of this that weight number stuck in my mind. I realize now that it became part of the trauma and I've been afraid to weigh that number ever since. Whenever I get close to that goal weight I literally have trouble breathing until I get my weight back up again. At least now I know what the problem is and I can slowly talk to myself about dealing with it. Turns out there was a good reason why I didn't want to weigh that number."

Winnie: "I was sexually abused as a kid and now I am fully aware that I have this weight on for protection. I don't really feel consciously like I need protection but doing this exercise I got in touch with the fact that I have a raving need to feel protected. But there are lots of ways to feel protected without the use of weight. I've been interested in martial arts but now I'm really motivated to take classes. If I felt that I could defend myself physically that would be a great, great gift I could give myself. I really feel that I wouldn't need this weight if I felt physically competent. I'm going for it!"

Sharon: "Everybody knew when I was thin that I was bulemic. I didn't keep it much of a secret. I got myself into a program and quit the habit. I gained all this weight. Now I realize that it is kind of my badge that says, 'See, I'm still not bulemic!' If I take the weight off everybody will think I've gone back to throwing up; they will think I lost that battle. I'm not sure what I'm going to do. Maybe just move away and start again somewhere else. And keep my mouth shut about the past."

Kathy: "I'm a minister's wife and that is a very social position. I love people. I love making an entrance into a room and getting hugs from everyone. I can hug every man in the room and nobody feels threatened because I am so huge. I can flirt outrageously and it's a lot of fun. I realize that my weight is working for me. If I were thin there's no way I'd be able to carry on like this! I know it's a strain on my body but I like things like they are. I guess I have to ask myself if flirting is worth it. I just feel like I'd have to change a lot in order to maintain a weight loss and quite frankly I don't know if I really want to. What is eye-opening to me is to understanding the dynamic of what's going on."

Bill: "People are very important to me too. I lost all my weight once and when I walked into the room nobody recognized me. Everybody seemed to give me a cold shoulder. I didn't feel like me any more. I felt introverted instead of extroverted. The weight came on after that night. I just had no idea that that experience haunted me so much. Now I'm in a completely different career, however, and nobody knows me anyway. Perhaps now I can take it off and not be so concerned about being recognized."

Mark: "My wife has a drug problem. I've steadily been gaining weight and I haven't been motivated to do anything about it. My wife says the weight is not attractive and I tell her 'your doing drugs is not attractive to me either'! We're locked in this and I know that my weight is somehow my way of telling her off. I've already told her 'you get off the drugs and I'll lose the weight' but I know this is nonsense. This marriage is over."

"All the answers you seek are within."
—Zen quote

Until these people "went within" none of them had the foggiest idea why they carried their weight—from 15 pounds to 150 extra pounds. The Inner Theatre technique provides a framework for getting to know yourself. These people all had a higher need—everything from having a reserve to fight cancer to the ability to flirt—only *now they know*. These are 15 different people with 15 different lives and 15 Very Good Reasons to be packing extra weight.

Having the weight on isn't a very creative solution to a problem when you think about it. It's a "standard design solution." At least 40 million people in the U.S. alone reach for it. Sure, it's working but in every one of those 15 stories, could you have come up with another way of dealing with the situation? Of course you could because you're outside the person. If you were inside, you might be stuck for a more creative answer too.

Sometimes talking to yourself and your inner parts is enough to solve the mystery. And sometimes you need to sign up for those karate lessons.

The Finale

Once you know the Very Good Reason or the "higher need" for your weight, you can understand the message or the benefit of the weight. The next step should be obvious: give yourself what the weight is giving you.

Is there any way that you can get what you want without having the weight on? When you meet that higher need, when you give yourself what you really, really want, the sabotaging behavior will fall away.

For some people, the weight keeps them out of situations that spell discomfort. For Denny, it meant a career change. For Patricia, it meant getting serious about assertiveness training. For Boker, it meant staying out of relationships that he didn't really want. For Cheryl it meant redefining "substance" in her work.

For many people having the weight on means never having to say "no." Not much is expected of a really fat person. Turning down invites to play softball, for instance, isn't a problem. As one overweight child said, "They don't expect as much from you."

How to Support Someone Who is Losing Weight

If you want to support your spouse, lover, kids or relatives with their weight loss, ask them, "How can I support you in this?" And then listen. Do what they say. You have to ask because different people want different kinds of support. Maybe what they'd really like is for you to shut up about it. Or maybe they'd appreciate it if you didn't bring cookies into the house for awhile. Or maybe they'd be tickled just to have you around to listen.

If you want to support co-workers with their weight loss, notice something positive about their *work*.

It is embarrassing to be acknowledged in the work environment for "body size," even if the comment is well intended. "Gee, you're looking good" is not something everyone likes to hear while working. For some, a comment like this may be so frightening that they gain the weight back. Not everybody wants to be attractive—and I mean that in its most literal sense. They don't want to attract attention (especially sexual attention) to themselves. Your "helpful" comments could be unnerving. Instead, an honest compliment about quality of work will go a long way to help self-confidence and also, a feeling that things are better.

Life Out of the Fat Lane

The world treats you differently at 210 pounds, 185 pounds, 145 pounds and 123 pounds. I know. I've been all those different weights. I wish someone had told me that yes, I would still have problems but they would be different problems. If I had just known that much, it would have helped.

Your life does not become perfect when the weight is gone. You still have clogged drains in your bathroom, your car still uses gas, bills still need to be paid. Losing the weight does not affect every aspect of your life. But I found that the world treated me differently. For one thing, people seemed to listen to me more and they gave me more credit for having some brains. This was a little unnerving at first. I discovered that I didn't have to prove myself so much in a business setting. People were more accepting of what I had to say.

I think that different kinds of men are attracted to different sizes of women.

It took less than one year to drop 100 pounds.

Just as I hit 124 pounds, one of the worst winters in history hit Chicago where I lived for two years. It was brutal weather and I learned something about fat: it keeps you warm. That first winter without my weight was painful. There was no amount of clothing that I could pile on that would stop the slicing wind of Lake Michigan.

Even now I use my electric blanket 11 months out of the year and I dress up to go to sleep. I have one of the world's greatest collection of socks. I'm the one who goes into Victoria's Secret and asks for "something provocative...with feet."

I still have the appetite of a Green Bay Packer. My taste buds still itch for the exotic. And I don't always feel like dealing with weight and food every day of my life. But, you know, success does not depend on how you feel. You don't have to like it, you just have to do it.

Questions and Answers

Q: Were you fat as a child?

I was a normal weight baby when I was born but by the time I was seven I weighed 102 pounds. Yes, I had the distinct misfortune to grow up as a "fat kid." I weigh less now than I did in the sixth grade. Children can be very cruel to each other. I was not only the fattest kid in school, I was also the tallest (until junior high school) and the *youngest* in every one of my classes. Unbeknownst to anyone I was also nearsighted which can cause a lot of grief when trying to go through a cafeteria line. You don't know what's up ahead so you take everything and then, of course, being a long-standing member of the Clean Plate Club, I ended up eating food I didn't even want!

Q: Did you use a group to lose the weight?

No. Overeaters Anonymous is an excellent program, however. I don't know anything about other groups because I have never participated. Do whatever works for you.

Q: Did you use drugs or surgery to lose the weight?

No. I recommend taking vitamins. I suspect that getting fully loaded with vitamins keeps cravings down. I keep my "bio-container" as satisfied as I can. I don't like depriving myself of anything.

Q: Have you ever been bulemic or anorexic?

Never.

Q: Did you exercise to lose the weight?

Exercise is great. It will help you take the weight off and keep it off and it is supposed to improve your disposition. I exercise now but I did not exercise during my big weight loss so the honest answer to this question is no.

Q: Did you have a bet with someone, use a partner or buy small size clothes as motivation?

No on all three counts. I did, however, have a picture of a very fat person posted on my refrigerator. Some people put a skinny person on their frig doors…that didn't work for me.

Q: What program did you go on?

I did not fast. I did not use canned, powdered or packaged diet plans of any kind. I did not use anybody's program. I did feel like I was starving much of the time. I know what it feels like to be very, very hungry—do you realize that most of the world's people are in this state daily? Now that I am older and more sensitive to blood sugar, I eat within 30 minutes of waking up and I do not let myself get hungry. Just a 1/2 cup of food will satisfy your hunger—you don't have to eat the whole cow!

Q: What don't you eat now?

If there is one "food" to eliminate it would be anything with alcohol in it. Forget the fact that it makes you fat, it makes you crazy…and unfortunately not just while you're drinking it either. It creates "stinking thinking" and causes me to make lousy food choices. Alcohol is metabolized as sugar. I avoid sugar. I have to say that if anyone told me I was going to have to give up sugar for the rest of my life, I would have seriously considered suicide. Instead, I was asked, "Can you leave sugar alone for 10 minutes?" And I could. And I did. Ten minutes turned into an hour, an hour turned into a day. A day became a week. Do you understand?

Q: How did you do it?

I negotiated with my Fat Person Within. Give up on what's "normal." Put yourself and your weight first. Do that now. Make it a problem you are determined to deal with. A priority. Get ornery. Get stubborn. Get creative. Figure out what it takes to take care of yourself. I am totally unique and so are you! Don't be afraid to be unconventional with your tactics. Stop being so concerned about what your behavior looks like to other people. This is killing you. When I lost the big weight I thought only in 5 pound increments. I'd say, "Wow, there's 195! The world didn't fall apart, let's see if we can go down to 190." I regarded taking the weight off like you might think of skindiving. I'd say, "Let's go down there (a weight number) and see what that's like."

Q: Did you get support from family and friends?

No. Family members frequently sabotage a weight loss. Figure out a way to deal with this and then do it. If someone in your family or your circle is having a problem with your weight loss, steer clear of them if you can.

Q: But every day, how do you do it *every day?*

I am not a person blessed with extraordinary willpower. Because of this I have had to be inventive, coming up with other ways of dealing with food, people, holidays, restaurants and all the rest of it. I am an ordinary person who got angry enough to say, "I want this for myself." Take very good care of yourself. Give yourself what you need to be happy and comfortable on this planet because nobody else is going to do it for you. And it's nobody else's job.

Q: What was your higher need? What was your very good reason?

It changed over the years. The reason I kept 15 pounds on was different than why I had 100 pounds on. I attended a lecture by a speaker who described the Miracle of the Cookie Jar. She said that when she worked very intensely and there was a batch of cookies in her cookie jar, she would eat them all. But when she allowed herself some play time, she noticed that she was satisfied with just one cookie. Most people treat play as an optional activity. I don't. Not any more. If I don't tend to my arthuring (my play time) *all the time,* I know the compulsion for food will overpower me. Play is a personal event. What is play for one person isn't necessarily play to another. For me, golf would be work.

What is play for you? Answering this question becomes paramount and needs to be treated with great respect. Think back to your kid days and remember what you liked to do then. Pick up where you left off. I like the play equipment at the neighborhood school yard. And I like any messy art projects whose end product is whimsical. This is not a sideline with me. It's a prescription for weight control and for a happy life. It is essential to me now.

Let's Wrap This Up!

An autopsy report indicated that health columnist Dr. Stuart Berger, 40, author of the popular 1985 book *Dr. Berger's Immune Power Diet,* died from a heart attack brought on by obesity. The 6'7" Berger, who in the early 1980's lost 210 pounds on his own diet, had ballooned back to 365 at the time of his death. **You must not forget that this weight thing can kill you.**

Wynona Judd: "My weight has been my protection from the outside world." **Protection is *by far* the most popular reason to have extra weight on.**

Comedian John Candy had a supportive family and a hot movie career but in the end (age 43), neither love nor money could save him from the weight problem he knew might be fatal. While his father's death at age 35 pushed Candy to strive for self-discipline, it also released in him a sense of fatalism: If he was doomed to die anyway, he seemed to reason, pass the potato chips. Eating, ingesting, smoking became a way of swallowing anxiety. **More people have committed suicide with a knife, fork and spoon that with any other weapon.**

Ballad of the Hungry I Cafe
(Advice to MySelf)

I think that I shall never see
An appetite as whacked as me.
I'm driven—like an Indy Racer
Sucking food with a coffee chaser.

I fuel myself for high protracking
When it's actually something I'm lacking.
I fuel up to meet the day
Not just to keep my hunger at bay.

A half a cup of food will do it
But I'll eat more and only rue it.
Then when I weigh me in the nude
I'll get the word on my choice of food.

I eat like a Viking warrior would
to take on the challenges that I should.
Then wake up from the battle later
To find that I've really been a traitor
To my ever lasting Battle Royal
I've done a lot, but not been loyal.

Fuel real hunger, that's OK!
Just leave it at that for the rest of the day!
To fight the fight I need to fight
I need to be calm and lean and light.
My Viking days of War are done
Relax, I think the Vikings won.

Lean tight buns are yours for dancing
Pass up bakery buns—not chancing.
Daily weapons needed, it's true,
But something other than food will do.

Dizzy with hunger? Yes, that's real
Eat then! If that's the deal...
But stuffing for a War—on what?
You really are some kind of nut!

Chapter 8
The Financial Sabotage

**"I don't really like money
but it quiets my nerves."**
—attributed to both Joe Lewis and Satchel Paige

Can you trust yourself with money? I couldn't. But I can now.

Do you sabotage your finances? Do you plan to save money and end up with debt instead? Do you think all you need is more money but you're already making good money now? Are there people making less money that you are who are debt-free and seem to have plenty? Where does your money go? Do you have the uneasy feeling that when you put cash in your wallet it somehow dissolves on its own?

Can you trust yourself with your finances? Do you control yourself with money and then blow it all on an impulse buy?

Self-esteem is feeling good about yourself even though you may be a lying, thieving flake.

Self-sabotage is when you say you want something and then go about making sure it doesn't happen.

Self-trust is when you can trust yourself with your own needs and desire for: weight loss, finances, exercise, work, play and relationships. Are you committed to your commitment?

Self-management is when you manage all internal aspects of yourself so no one part goes wanting.

Self-discipline is when you focus on a mission to the exclusion of other missions.

Will having money make you a better person? Probably not. If you're a good person now, you'll still be a good person with $200,000 in the bank.

Are you a bad person if you don't have money? Certainly not. Do only good people have money? Certainly not. Having money or not having money is not the issue here. What is at issue is this:

____yes ____no Do you have a goal to have money and then sabotage that goal?

____yes ____no Are you personally happy with how you handle money?

I'm not here to give you a goal about money. What you do with money is your own personal business. If you're not happy with your behavior with money, however, I'm here to crack the code of behavior if you sabotage your finances. (If you answered "yes" and "no" in that order above.)

> ## "The hard part about being broke is watching the rest of the world go buy."
> —Alan F.G. Lewis

Small business owners are a nervous bunch if they believe in statistics. Eight out of ten small businesses fail. "Do you ever get over the fear?" one entrepreneur asked me as we were preparing the second stage of her marketing plan. "Nope, it's always there and you get so used to it that after a while if it wasn't there, you'd miss it," I answered.

The owner of a helicopter service was being interviewed by a newspaper reporter who asked, "Does being an entrepreneur still make you nervous?" and she answered, "Yes, I still have butterflies but now they fly in formation."

There's nothing wrong with fear if it propels you into positive action.

> ## "Fear is just excitement in need of an attitude adjustment."
> —Russ Quaglia and Doug Hall

If your fear of injury causes you to buckle up in your car, is this such a bad thing? If your fear of burglars makes you lock your door at night where's the negative there? If your fear of running out of money when you're 90 causes you to get serious about financial planning, this is a good thing, right? Fear is a motivator. Fear can be voices from the future telling you that if you don't face facts (about weight or money or relationships), you're looking at ten miles of rough road ahead.

Do you worry about money? I used to worry about money incessantly. I worried more than I *breathed.* My internal Financial Director was a mean-spirited taskmaster that I'd take pleasure in circumventing. This part of me was about as flexible as The Terminator and had all the charm of Nurse Ratchet on testosterone. Full of "should's" "must's" "have to's" and "ought to's" this internal part was just asking to be sabotaged. The continual conversation in my head seemed to be a litany of "I want" followed by "You can't have." The Financial Director said "no" to everything. I seemed to delight in sabotaging this part.

I've sat through prosperity workshops and religiously applied the affirmation techniques. I understood that I was not my bank account and that my self-worth was not measured in dollars and cents. I got all that, OK? I rehearsed the line about the lilies of the field and how they didn't concern themselves with money. They know the Universe will take care of them...why didn't I have such faith? None of this helped. What was wrong with me that I couldn't stop obsessing about my finances? Somehow if I was spiritually in tune I would release my death grip on the material world.

And what was I to do with this overload of *wants?* Wants seem to scream from every pore! I wanted home repair, glitz, European travel, college courses, money to give to great causes, a hot tub, really healthy food, appliances, play tickets, sports equipment and someone to clean my house and yard. And then there was the never-ending temptation of street rods and antique cars. I seemed to want everything I saw.

"Whatever problem I had,
I knew I had two options: eat or buy something.
Usually I did both."
—Louie Anderson in *Goodbye Jumbo*

It doesn't take a genius to see a parallel here to food. I wanted all the food and I wanted all the stuff and like a good Baby Boomer, I wasn't particularly willing to wait for satisfaction. I failed New Age 101 where you convinced yourself that these things were not real, would not give you lasting pleasure and that you should talk yourself out of wanting them. If I had my spiritual act together, the desire for a '34 Ford roadster would simply fall away. Instead I'd want the simple pleasures of incense (10 sticks for $2), candles ($38 for the aroma therapy ones), a personal home fountain ($178 with self-cleaning pump) and a clear crystal spear point ($100) to place next to my teak meditation bench ($73) and of course, the yoga and what's-new-on-the-New-Age-Hit-Parade classes for this month. Once I connected with Spirit and had all my senses awakened (the truly enlightened Life) then I could put the newly awakened Alyce into my very own sensory deprivation tank ($7,000). What actually happened was I ended up wanting the car, the candles, the classes and renting the tank.

The Sunday newspaper fueled my compulsion. The ads set me off like Orson Wells at a buffet line. I'd see something that I had to have at that fabulous price. I *must* have it! This is too good to pass up! Only problem was, these great opportunities happened *every* Sunday.

I seemed to be a master at getting rid of money. I could blow it away faster than anybody. It was there and it was gone as if I was waving magic dust over it. And this all happened so fast that I was mystified. Any of this sounding at all familiar?

If you have the unnerving feeling that money explodes or dissolves or mysteriously disintegrates while in your possession and you have spent more than $70 in your lifetime on zen books, then welcome to the fascinating world of Financial Sabotage.

**"There's a certain Buddhistic calm
that comes from having money in the bank."**
—Tom Robbins

It is entirely possible that you are not going to feel comfortable on this planet until you have some money salted away some where. You may be the kind of person that there is no amount of medication or meditation that will let you accept life without bucks. What you require is a little Green Valium.

What is your relationship with money?

How do you talk to yourself about money?

Go back even further. How did others talk about you and money?

"The only person who seemed to enjoy money as much as I was my grandfather," wrote one woman writer. "Unlike my mother, he treated money *without apology*. Handling money made my mother anxious and she raised me never to discuss the price of anything. As much as I hated being different, I wanted money more."

We all have a relationship with money. It is as if it is a character on stage with us.

"I have enough money to last me the rest of my life, unless I buy something."
—Jackie Mason

Watch how you treat money. When you pay for something, do you set the bills down for the clerk to take or do you hold the paper out for them to take it from your hand? How do you receive money? Isn't it interesting that our paychecks are delivered in envelopes and placed face down on a desk? When you leave a tip do you hide it under a plate? We speak of "dirty money" and money that "gets laundered."

Everyone knows that "money is the root of all evil." Wrong. What the line actually said was, *"The desire for money is the root of all evil."* Money as a thing has no good or evil to it. It's like fire or energy—it depends on what you do with it.

You'll have a more difficult time of getting more of it if you think it's dirty or is going to cause you harm. Does that seem obvious? Do you rejoice when money comes your way?

Who do you like to give money to? Small children, right? Because they haven't learn to stifle their enthusiasm yet. Their faces light up like Christmas tree bulbs when you hand them money. Your face should do the same. "I rejoice when money arrives."

Some people believe that money attracts money—literally. So they carry a $100 bill, not to be spent, but as a magnet for other money to find them. I thought this was an interesting notion so I tried it. And for me, the $100 bill found ways to evaporate right along with the $20 and $1's! But I still thought the concept had merit, so I kept a handsome 100 mark note from a trip to Germany in with my American money. It had the denomination 100 clearly on it and it was definitely money, just not easily spent. The blue Deutsche mark went through the laundry a couple of times literally. I accidentally washed it. It became so dog-eared that I finally laminated it. I still have it so possibly the magic of this practice works. Although how it knows to attract *money* and not actual *Germans* is still a mystery.

If someone swore to me that turning around three times before getting into bed would insure financial wealth, I'd probably try that too. And if it worked, I'd keep doing it! I'd do it to illustrate *to myself* that I really *don't* want to sabotage my finances. I really do want to be financial solvent and responsible with money and I'm willing to do whatever it takes including being unconventional to accomplish this.

Many years ago when my struggle with money was at its height I was talking to my parents long distance and I asked them about their mothers. It became an interview that changed my perspective about money. Both of my grandmothers, as it turns out, were good money managers. My mother's mother had ten kids and found herself widowed living on a farm in the Dust Bowl and in the middle of the Great Depression. Sell the farm? Who in their right mind would buy it? And yet, when she died at the age of 97, my grandmother left thousands of dollars to her offspring. How on earth did she do it? My father's widowed mother, when it was time for her daughter to go to college, moved to the college town, bought a large house with many bedrooms which she rented out and *lived in the basement*. She eventually felt solvent enough to occupy the first floor of the house and continued to rent out every conceivable space to college students. Both her children earned college degrees. What a remarkable idea! What parent today would think to go along with their kid to college and do such a plan?

What I learned from interviewing my parents is the remarkable creativity both grandmothers had when it came to financing what they wanted. I recommend that everyone look to stories of their grandparents rather than their parents for inspiration. I desperately needed a good role model for money management and I found it two generations back.

There will be over 1 million bankruptcies filed in the United States this year. (Source: Administrative Office of the U.S. Courts) Will one of them be yours?

Would you consider it environmental pollution to throw paper out of your car window? You regard litter bugs as pretty trashy people, don't you? Then why do you think any less of those who pollute the economic environment? People who bounce checks, don't honor their financial commitments and go bankrupt are polluting commerce.

With the exception of bankruptcies resulting from health care problems, most are preventable. But just like obesity, people head straight for it like they're on runaway freight trains. Some pretty nice people have gone bankrupt. They've taken even nicer people down with them. You'll get a lot of attention for this behavior. Lawyers and bankers and IRS agents who ordinarily wouldn't give you the time of day are now giving you a call. Perhaps your family has gathered around you during this devastating time. Maybe you got bailed out and the person helping you just got extra polish on their halos for it. Isn't financial chaos fun?

I grew up in a family that moved on a regular basis. I saw that my father was the money earner and not my mother. In my simplistic kid mind I also saw that my father's work decided where and when we would move, not my mother's. I somehow got the impression from this that the person with the money got to make the rules. If I wanted to be the one making the rules, that would mean that I would have to be the one making the money. I also saw money as a channel of energy and I could funnel little streams of it in different directions. Some of it could actually be saved.

As a kid I did receive an allowance. If certain chores were done, I'd receive $2 a month. I was admonished for having that much money until I made the trip to the little brick bank downtown and deposited it into a savings account. Once a year I might be allowed to draw a little out to buy presents for other family members. This continued for several years until my little worn bank book read $52, a miniature fortune in my eyes. Then the family was once again moved.

When we had been in our new station for a couple of months I remembered my bank account and in a panic I told my mother that my money had been left behind. She said that "no" it wasn't and that she had received it when she closed all the accounts at the bank. OK. Then where was my $52? It had somehow been absorbed into the family money and no longer was tagged with my name. I never saw the money, nor was a new account ever set up. I had to just forget about it. And I thought that I had.

Until 20 years later I was a struggling 30-year old with a daughter of my own. I had a mortgage, electric bills, an obligation to buy dog food and school supplies. I had all the outward appearances of being a responsible adult but money, cash especially, seemed to vanish. I was dumbfounded as to its location once it was in my possession. The speed of its exit was truly remarkable.

To slow down this speed and to help solve the mystery I decided to write down everything, every *thing* that I spent costing more than 25 cents. This was the enlightening exercise that I needed. It slowed the process down as if filming a shooting bullet with high speed film. Now I could see the impact. Now I could see my behavior in slow motion and only then could I advise myself to change.

I couldn't seem to make the connection that a rectangular piece of plastic was actually dollars going out. It just didn't feel like I was spending money so I cut up one department store credit card. Until I could grasp that, I took myself off the card. The next thing I did was cancel the Sunday newspaper where all the marvelous "savings" were to be had. I figured that whatever bargains were out there that I was supposed to have, they'd have to find me another way. I also decided that I could not invest in the entertaining of others. Being a social hostess was, at that point, beyond my means and I needed to put the money elsewhere, like in my daughter's college fund.

Sometime during this period I asked myself what my upbringing had been with money. Why wasn't I a natural saver of money? Why did part of me seem so bent on spending it? It was only then that I remembered the infamous $52 left behind in a little brick bank in Missouri. I discovered that part of me was still pretty miffed about the money. I'd been such a diligent saver and what did I have to show for it? This kid part of me felt that if *I spent it,* I'd have *stuff* and that was better than putting the money in a bank where it would disappear. I realized that I had hit emotional pay dirt when I felt the feelings of money loss.

I tried to reason with myself about the $52. That was then, this is now. You're an adult and you're in control. These were just words, my kid part said. No amount of convincing me was working. A bank was a place that took your money and gave it away to someone else, my kid part pointed out. Denying myself the pleasure of spending the money for all those long kid years had resulted in nothing. So now, by heaven's, I'd had something to show for it—I'd buy stuff with it! I was getting no where with my financial sabotage. Time to grow up and stop being silly about $52. I couldn't convince my kid part that she was wrong—because she *wasn't wrong.*

Then I did an unusual thing. I called my mother one day and asked for my $52 back. She, of course, had no recollection of my bank account from years ago but fortunately she didn't deny that yes, she had probably taken it. She and my dad were what you might call "well-heeled" at that point and although my mother regarded this whole conversation as a little weird, she sent me $52 in cash. Cash, green stuff was what I put in the bank and it was green stuff that I needed to see back. When the money arrived, I put it in a plastic sleeve and hung it on my home office wall. I needed to have my kid part see that the money was back (maybe not with interest, but it was *back!)* and that putting money in a bank was an OK thing to do. Now isn't this a ridiculous story?

Yeah, but it worked. That $52 was the most important $52 of my adult life. I still have it. My internal kid part can see it, touch it and play with it and even spend it but I no longer feel ripped off. I'm no longer controlled by a compulsion that insists on spending the money before anyone else can get to it. I no longer *have* to spend money. I can do other things with it now, like save it or invest it. I enjoy keeping track of it and watching the numbers change into bigger numbers.

Do I wish that I could have been more "mature" about the $52? Sure. Did asking for the money seem childish and embarrassing? You betcha it did! Did I want to get over my financial sabotage? Yes, more than anything! Was I finally taking care of business without regard to how it would look to anybody else? Affirmative!

> **"Money is a funny thing.**
> **Any amount you don't have,**
> **whether it's $50 or $500,000**
> **will appear to be a mountain."**
> —Unknown

I was a guest on a radio talk show one morning and the topic was self-sabotage and procrastination. The broadcast room was typical, a small space full of equipment including large speakers the size of Volkswagens suspended from the ceiling. After an insightful little discussion with the talk show host, the lines were open for callers. They all wrestled with the usual procrastination problems but one woman caller made a huge impression on everybody.

"I put off paying my bills," she said. "I mean, I put off paying them until they disconnect the electricity and shut off the phone. And I don't really understand why I do this because I have the money to pay. I just don't do it."

What fascinating behavior! I said to her, "I don't know why you do it either but let's try this on for size...when you were a kid, did your mom ever say to you, 'Now play nicely with the other children. Share your toys'?"

The woman's voice roared out of those Volkswagen speakers! "Ohhhhhh, I hated that!" she yelled. When the DJ and I only slightly recovered our hearing I said to her, "Try on the idea that your money is your toys. When a bill arrives…what's your reaction?"

"I don't have to and you just try to make me," the woman replied.

Well, fine. Who's being harmed by this rebellion? The phone company doesn't care if she's rebelling. The electric and the gas company, they don't care. This adult woman was using her money and clutching it because of a higher need to rebel. As a rebellion, it wasn't all that effective. But until she called the station that day, she was literally locked into this behavior and mystified by it. So we talked about other ways to rebel. Write letters to the newspaper. Walk in demonstration marches. Post your political views on lawn signs. Plaster a rebellious slogan on the bumper of your car. Create a web site. There are lots of way to rebel that don't involve bill paying. Our conversation wasn't finished until she had a strategy for meeting her higher need for rebellion.

Notice that at no point did I try to *talk her out of rebelling*. She had a need to rebel, honor that, encourage that, revel in it! How can we express even more rebellion! There's nothing wrong with rebellion. The United States was founded on it! We think our forefathers were grand men for throwing tea in the harbor. Hurrah for rebellion! Rebellion is not the problem to be "fixed" here and she didn't need "fixing." All that was needed was to have the higher need identified (which was a lucky first guess on my part) and honored. Now she was free to expression her rebellion and pay her bills on time.

Stop saying you "can't afford it." If your mind hears you saying that, it will make sure that you will never have enough money. Instead, recognize that you can afford it (whatever it is) and that you are choosing not to spend the money this way at this time. You may say, "I can't afford a trip to Paris," when the truth is, "I'm spending my money on a new truck instead." It's not "I can't afford a new truck" but rather "I don't want to go into debt for a new truck." "I'd rather pay my bills than travel to Paris." Tell yourself the truth about money.

> **"We put off what we want most for what we want at the moment."**
> —Anonymous

This certainly holds true for the food...it's doubly true for the financial plan. I have a part of me that I call Oligb. Oligb is the Old Lady I'm Gonna Be. Oligb is a feisty old character who isn't going to want to scrimp and certainly isn't going to want to ask anybody else for money. She will want to maintain her independence and live in her own house and give money to the charities she chooses. I can tell she will like having a *lot* of money. I think about Oligb nearly every day and she advises me on how to manage my money now. I am hoping that Oligb is being influenced by my efficient grandmothers. I have made friends with Oligb and we rarely complain to each other any more about finances. She locks horns with my investment advisor from time to time but he knows she's there and even he addresses her specifically on occasion. To take care of Oligb I have divided my lot into an "A" account and a "B" account. Oligb has forbidden me from using any money in her account. We understand each other. When I actually become Oligb, I will probably thank my Past Self every day for the wonderful life I have.

Have you ever done something nice for your future self? Something simple like lay out the clothes you're going to wear for the next day? Have you made the deviled eggs for the picnic the day *before* so that you wouldn't be rushed? Have you requested the special meal on the plane for that trip next month? Then it is not a great leap for you to consider your own Oligb or Omigb. If you fail to plan are you really planning to fail?

> **"The only sure way to double your money is to fold it and put it back in your pocket."**
> —Anonymous

Know when I finally stopped worrying about money? When I:
   a) had some.
   b) realized I never got paid any money for worrying.
   c) both.
The answer is c.

I was in a hammock one day worrying about money when I had the Big Ah-ha. As I lay rigidly in the green canvas hammock listening to the internal talk show of my mind, I heard an interesting opinion. "You have never been paid a dime to worry." What? I grasped it.

I get paid for showing up, for physically arriving at a work place and being there nine hours. Most Americans operate under this directive. I get paid to listen, talk, write and physically do my job—at that time it was managing people, equipment and resources. When I wasn't right there at the office, when I was instructing night classes, I also got paid for teaching which was more listening, talking and writing. All of this activity was done in exchange for salary, compensation, a pay check, in short, money. At no time was I ever given any money for the mental activity of *worrying*.

So I decided that I like getting paid for what I do. There was no point in doing anything, in fact for me there was no *time* to do anything that I didn't get paid for. At no time did I earn any money worrying. All of a sudden worrying didn't make a lot of sense. It wasn't putting any more money where I needed it.

My friend Gary has gained and lost a million dollars twice and he's on his third try at being a millionaire. Do you suppose he'll be able to keep it this time?

I know a woman who has gained and lost 100 pounds three times! She is on her way back down. Do you suppose she'll be able to keep it off this time?

Until the higher need is addressed, until the code of this behavior is cracked, both people are doomed to repeat their spectacular behavior patterns. Neither person is stupid. And neither do they understand their behavior. In both cases a higher need is being met. His higher need is to not have money and her higher need is to have the weight.

**"The upper crust is a group of crumbs
held together by dough."**
—Joseph A. Thomas

What is your internal reaction to this quote?

What higher need is being served by not having money? If there is a benefit to mismanaging money and not having it around, what could that benefit be? Here's a list of possible reasons to sabotage finances:

… to be rescued.

… to punish (you don't deserve a good life for some perceived past offense).

… to stay connected to family or social group (could you show up in a Rolls Royce and not feel guilty?) to keep yourself in a constant state of terror.

… to live up to the perception that you are lousy with money (somebody told you that you were bad with money and you can't prove them wrong).

… you believe that if you're rich that you'll also be stingy, miserable, preyed upon or stuck up (see quote above).

… you buy into the "money is the root of all evil" concept.

… you think that if you're successful getting money and then lose it, you'll be labeled a dolt.

… you have to have something to worry about because a person without something to worry about is not an important person.

… if you have money that means somebody else doesn't have it; you buy into the scarcity idea of money.

… you divide the world into have's and have not's and your social group regards the have's with disdain (see quote above).

… the getting of the thing, the pursuit is more pleasurable than the actual having of it.

… you know that no matter what you do "wrong" with money someone will come along and make it right for you (akin to rescuing).

More than one parent has been afraid to let junior know if they have money because if junior knew, junior would be asking for it. I met one woman who was trying to make a success of a boat business and yet sabotaged it. It took a near financial capsizing for her to come to the shocking realization that if she had money, she knew her *parents* would want it! She felt she had no internal resources to say "no" to a money request. She had the double whammy of feeling that she would lose respect for them if they *did* ask!

What would you do if you had money?

If you said, "Wow! I'd travel!" and there's a part of you that is scared to death to travel, doesn't it make perfect sense that this part would make sure that you never had enough money? If you answered, "I'd get married!" and there's a part of you protecting you from having a long term relationship, doesn't it make perfect sense that this part will keep you from earning too much money?

> **"All I want is a chance to prove**
> **that having a lot of money**
> **will not make me miserable."**
> —Anonymous

If you recognize that you are sabotaging your finances, you need to acknowledge that part of you that is protecting you from having money. This part of you is serving a higher need. If you want to change how you deal with this part of yourself, you can. The result will be a negotiated peace within you about your finances.

Get a paper and pen or sit at a word processor. Ask to speak to the part of you that is responsible for your present financial condition.

When this person identifies themselves, thank them and ask if they will be willing to work with you on this situation.

When they acknowledge, thank them and proceed as outlined in the chapters entitled, "The Course." Then ask:

Of what benefit are you to me?

What higher need do you have for me?

What do you protect me from?

What do you think is best for me?

What advantage is financial chaos serving for me?

Is there something that I get to *stay connected to* by sabotaging my money?

Discover your higher need, understand the higher need and meet it.

Examples:

Can you have money and not alienate your family?

- If you say "yes," then how exactly, specifically will you do that?
- Vividly imagine circumstances that will arise and how you will handle these situations.
- Are you heavily invested in rebellion and your counterculture lifestyle requires you to be poor but you want money anyway? Is there a way to serve both needs? In what way, *specifically,* can you do both?
- To be an artist, do you think you have to be a Starving Artist?
- Does your fear of success keep you from excelling financially? Do you think there may be a way of **continuing to have the fear but get a handle on your finances anyway?** Can they exist together? Would you be willing to just feel the fear, let it be there and be a good money manager anyway? Is there some other area you could be a failure that would satisfy this need and not affect your money?

One of the wealthiest men in Washington State couldn't bring himself to buy a Cadillac. He felt that such a car would distance him from his working class employees. He himself had come up through the ranks and had become the C.E.O. He drove a Buick and as the car began to wear out he went shopping for a replacement Buick. Buick no longer made the large sized sedans but Cadillac did. He continued to drive his beloved Buick knowing that time was running out on it. I finally suggested that he buy a new Cadillac and have the emblems taken off and replaced with Buick emblems. A good body shop could redesign the Caddie's distinctive tail lights and *voila!* he'd have the car he wanted. You may think that this true story is a little nuts, but what would it take for *you to meet your higher need and be a millionaire too?*

"It's not hard to meet expenses, they're everywhere."
—internet humor

A Chicago-based psychotherapist writes, "I always look for what the payoff is for any roadblocking behavior. People must be getting something they need out of their failures and frustrations or they wouldn't continue to be failures." Interestingly, she says, many people discover that they're blocking their own success because they're afraid of surpassing their parents' status in the world.

What happens if you reach success beyond that of your parents? Often, you're abandoned by that parent, who feels jealous of your success and no longer plays a supportive role. Albert Brooks starred as a writer stumped with his own sabotage in a movie with Debbie Reynolds as his closet writing mother. The pushing and pulling of her on-again off-again support and non-support of his writing didn't make sense until he discovered *her* writing hidden in a box. In this situation, it is easy to see why each step a person takes towards success can alienate you further from your family.

"I believe that the power to make money
is a gift from God."
—John D. Rockefeller

What if he's right? What if your ability to find, make, create and hold wealth was considered a gift—like the gift of being able to make beautiful music with a violin? Wouldn't you feel a bit of an obligation to care for that talent or at least honor it and encourage it?

Just like with the weight, once you have negotiated a successful settlement within yourself on your issue, you will no longer have to bird dog your behavior. You won't have to be on guard, stealing yourself against your own sabotage. If you've been honest and discussed your higher need, then you've cracked the code and now you can trust yourself with your finances.

Chapter 9
Procrastination:
The Time Sabotage

**"Procrastination is suicide
on the installment plan."**
—Anonymous

Procrastination.
I love to do it.
I must.
I do it all the time.
I'm so good at it; I can even do it in my sleep.
Mostly I can do it when I'm in love.
'Cause I love to do it.
To say I will and then won't.
It's a lot like loving.
'Cause given the option I'll leave.
And wander off to do my Life.
I'll do it slow or I'll do it fast.
But I will do my Life exactly unaccording to my plan.
Procrastination is more important than sex.
It must be. We do it more often.

What on earth could be easier than just putting it off? We can be Baby Boomers or Gen X's, nonconformists, machinists, capitalists, purists, racists, podiatrists, botanists, contortionists, realists, cartoonists or atheists—we all procrastinate. We all talk to ourselves about it and then do it *anyway*.

Procrastination does not discriminate and it's extremely versatile. It affects men and women equally and every race and religion. It is cross cultural. It is also portable, compact, has no moving parts, requires no training, one size seems to fit all and it can be literally hazardous to your health.

"My sister died of that," a woman told me after a self-sabotage seminar I led in Canada. I was momentarily stunned by her statement and she went on, "My sister had cancer. They operated on her and said if you have any of the following symptoms get back to us. She had the symptoms and she put off going back and put it off longer and longer until she died."

So procrastination is not simply this annoying thing that we inject into our lives. That's what I thought when I wrote the *The Time Sabotage* (aka the *Procrastinator's Success Kit)* in 1986. Since then people have shared stories with me of devastated lives, sabotaged health, wrecked marriages and destroyed businesses all due to procrastination. Muppet creator Jim Henson put off going to the hospital by a mere five hours and died as a result of an ordinary, treatable infection. Cary Grant put off going to the hospital *while he was having a heart attack.*

Procrastination is our favorite form of self-sabotage. It is available and convenient. It is also a creative response to our environment.

**"If you want to spend tomorrow being
glad you did it,
you have to do it today."**
—Unknown

April 15th fascinates me. Every year the local news media starts gathering at the main Post Office around 10 P.M. The traffic jam of cars extends in all directions. Late tax filing citizens with fat envelopes in hand join the annual parade, sit in idling SUV's in long lines trying to reach the Post Office by the Cinderella hour. The TV news people interview these classic procrastinators. A local pizza place provides free pizza. By 11 P.M. it turns into a street party. Excitement begins to crackle in the air as the minute by minute count down is reported somewhat similar to New Year's Eve. Postal workers are stationed around the main drop off boxes and take envelopes from the people in the cars. People greet each other, laugh and smile and wave. It finally becomes clear that some people at the end of the line aren't going to make it. And I think to myself, "It is as if the deadline of April 15 was just established this year." What is fascinating about this whole scene is that it happens *every year.* And every year there will be the same scene. I'm here to tell you right now that April 15 will occur in this next year. It should not be a surprise. There should be no reason to wait in line, idling your engine and hoping you'll make it. But I look at the scene and I think, "if I didn't know what was going on I'd think this was a celebration of some sort." This is kinda fun. You get free pizza, your neighbors get to see you on TV and when are you ever treated so royally by the Post Office? This coming April 15th there will be another big city block party and there will be literally thousands of people who will act as if they didn't know that date was on their calendars.

Procrastination is not the evil, laziness that you thought that is was. It is not a cruel joke that you play on yourself either. Instead, procrastination is an effective way to handle your stay on this planet. It is an option. You may be ready to try other ways to living your life, however. Procrastination is a *choice* and it may be one that you're ready to stop using right now knowing, of course, that you can pick it up again later.

Does this sound a little radical to you? I hope so. Because the conventional methods aren't working.

Subconsciously, in our heart of hearts, we know that we can't do everything. Knowing this, we select what we're going to do. What we unconsciously select to do has little connection with what we say we're going to do. In fact, the distance between words and actions is about 12 inches between our heads and our hearts.

There are lots of different ways to enjoy your stay on this planet. One of the tools for dealing with life is certainly procrastination.

Telling yourself to just stop procrastinating is a useless conversation. Beating ourselves up with internal lectures is annoying and offers no results. Self-help pep talks offer little help. Time management is a graceful art form and if you don't know the techniques, you learn them. But if you're going to sabotage your time management program anyway, learning more will be a waste of time.

Procrastination is a message to you from a part of You that wants something. Your job is to receive that message and then to decode it.

Recognize the benefit or pay value of your procrastination and then give yourself that benefit. The procrastinating behavior will fall away. It's just that simple. Not *easy,* simple.

Dogs don't procrastinate. A dog does not say, "There's that cat. I'll go bite that cat next Tuesday." They get up and they go bite the cat! You used to be that way. When you were two years old and you saw a cookie, did you say to yourself, "Do I deserve it? Would I be disturbing anybody if I asked for it?" *NO!* You said, "Cookie now!" You used to be this way but now you procrastinate. What does that tell you? It tells you that this is a *learned* behavior and it can be unlearned or something learned in its place. It means that you're not stuck with it! This should be the best news you've heard all week!

"I should do my life while I'm thinking about it."
—Robert Selby

When procrastinating becomes a way of life, it can interfere with job performance, affect professional and personal relationships and can cause anxiety and depression.

Are you sick and tired of your procrastinating? Are you willing to be unconventional to solve this problem?

If you are procrastinating, you're in good company. Demonsthenes shaved one side of his head so that he would be ashamed to be seen in public and therefore stop procrastinating on practicing his oration skills. Procrastinating French novelist Victor Hugo ordered his servants to confiscate his clothes until he finished his writing assignments.

Some people have to be in a lot of pain before they will look at solving a problem. This isn't necessary but they do it anyway. Life can be like riding an elevator. You don't have to hit bottom, however, in order to make a behavioral change. If you got in the elevator on the 20th floor and that's when this behavior started, you can stop the elevator and get off on the 11th floor or the 5th floor. You don't have to ride the thing all the way down. You can get off before it gets worse.

In a culture that worships success and overachieving, it is difficult to believe that procrastination can be anything positive. But in a culture that values *results,* procrastination becomes an understandable champion. How could putting things off get results?

Well, what results do you want?

What better way to get sympathy from your co-workers than to wait until the last minute to finish that report? What better way to keep people at a distance than to procrastinate about maintaining relationships? Could there be any easier way to add drama to your life than running the deadline out? What better way is there to hide your potential than to continue slam dunking projects at the last minute? And what more socially acceptable way is there to rebel against your spouse or your employer than putting off what you said you were going to do?

Procrastination protects us. It helps us tolerate impossible environments. It's convenient and easy-to-learn. Few human activities can compare with the genius of procrastination. Putting everything off to the last minute is an insidious way of blocking success by making it impossible to do anything exceptionally well. You condemn yourself to the ordinary.

Guilt is the constant companion of the procrastinator. Guilt is a feeling. Procrastination, however, is an *action* (or lack of action) and your feelings about it are up to the you.

There was a successful man who received regional attention from scores of professional people simply by procrastinating. His repeated acts of putting things off resulting in offers from his girlfriend and his parents to save his financial neck. He could never seem to get things done on time whether it was a business proposal or household tasks. He went bankrupt, of course, and got plenty of attention for that. He continues to run on a time clock that is about 23 hours off kilter. His ex-partners and ex-spouses gather every now and then to toast their good fortune at having outlived their disasters with him. The I.R.S. comes around to make house calls and his kids have learned to take reliable public transportation.

This man is a creative genius. He orchestrates his relationships to keep people at a comfortable distance while maintaining dependent rescue missions with others. He is an excellent example of how you too can improve the quality of stress in your life and in the lives of everyone around you.

How we use procrastination to get what we want is a completely different way of looking at this baffling behavior. Procrastinating on decisions and commitments can make you feel less helpless in situations where someone else may have the power. Procrastination can help you gain acceptance by your peers when you begin to look too successful. And if you work in a large corporation and you procrastinate, there are two things that will likely happen:

1. No one will notice.
2. Someone will come up with information that will cause a directive that will make the task unnecessary anyway.

People are never more creative than when they're sabotaging their own efforts and often never more productive than when they are procrastinating.

Who was running the bicycle shop while the Wright brothers were at the beach in North Carolina with their kites and aeroplanes? And which commissioned painting got postponed while Leonardo da Vinci sketched ideas for the helicopter?

It's amazing how many things you can get done while you're avoiding doing whatever it is that you said you were going to do.

For a disciplined person, there are two possible outcomes:

1. You get there.
2. You don't get there.

For a procrastinator, there are also two possible outcomes:

1. After much agonizing, you don't get there.
2. After much agonizing, you get there.

We're looking at a Quality of Life issue here. Are you ready to experience it?

"Show me what you do," said the sage, "and I will show you your life." Show me what you avoid and I will show you your internal genius, says Alyce.

THE ACTION JUNKIE PROCRASTINATOR

We'll start with this one because it is the most obvious. If all the calendars and timepieces in the world were suddenly destroyed, most of us would be grateful for 15 minutes, then we'd be bored. We love deadlines. In fact, most of us can't get motivated without one. If the microwave doesn't work fast enough for you, you may be an Action Junkie Procrastinator.

"I work well under pressure."
—cartoon character in a canon

Creative procrastination provides drama in our lives. Most of us can't stand to have things running too smoothly for very long and procrastination provides excitement and pressure that we all need. In fact, some people just can't feel important without it.

I worked for a corporate vice-president who had the Mr. Dithers Syndrome. Every morning at nine o'clock he would explode like Dagwood's boss. He had the perspective that in order to be seen as important, one must have problems. If the problems were big enough then you were very, very important. (Perhaps you had a parent who bought into this syndrome.)

If you don't happen to have any immediate problems you can procrastinate and develop some, like putting off doing your taxes until April 14. The result will be that you, and frequently people around you, will be catapulted into Action Land. Things are more dramatic here, some think that things are actually more creative here.

I'm not here to talk to you out of your procrastination. It's much more enlightening to figure out what you're getting for this behavior and then give yourself that! If your higher need is for action, then by all means, get more action in your life.

There's lots of ways of doing that. You can play the stock market, take up driving a cab in New York City, babysit small children or take up skydiving.

When I suggested this in a seminar to a group of people who all worked for the same bank, everyone turned and looked at this one fellow. I stopped and asked, "What's the deal here?"

The fellow answered: "I didn't realize it but it was pointed out to me that my procrastination was causing problems here at work." Everyone around the table nodded in agreement. "So," he continued, "I decided that if that was what it was, I'd get more action. I took up skydiving."

"And did that work?" I asked. He didn't have to answer! Everyone else in the room was nodding in the affirmative!

So this one's been field tested.

Some people get off on their own adrenaline. Adrenaline is a drug. It's like giving yourself a shot of power. It's stimulating. Continued use and abuse, however, like most drugs, begins to look like addiction.

A woman vice-president of a computer hardware company: "No matter how successful I get, my mother has bigger problems or has a bigger cause than I have. It took me 20 years to realize how competitive she is and how exaggerated she makes her life. She doesn't have a headache, she has a brain tumor. She escalates everything as some kind of self-motivation. Now that I recognize this I can watch for it and correct it in myself."

Stress without distress is motivation.

There are probably more Action Junkie Procrastinators in the media than anywhere else. That's logical, isn't it? Any place you find deadlines, you're likely to find people who are attracted and motivated by them.

Doug was a city planner and projects in his life had ten and fifteen year completion spans. When he was given ten days to prepare for a presentation for a citizens meeting, he frittered away a week before starting. "I even loafed on the weekend," he described. "I got up at 4 A.M. Monday morning to begin drawing up the charts for the meeting. I felt absolutely alive. The whole thing came together. It felt great to have something that would have a beginning, a middle and an end. I relished it. Ordinarily I wouldn't act this way. There was no margin for error, no chance to come down with a cold or be distracted with anyone else's problems (like my wife's). I loved having that kind of focus."

Focus, by the way, is the number one trait of winners. They have the ability to focus on whatever they have picked as a win. Doug made it a personal goal to get involved with faster moving projects and eventually even changed careers.

Lance Armstrong won the grueling Tour de France bicycle race after winning a successful battle with cancer. Interviewed on television he said, "I don't think I could have won the race if I hadn't had cancer. Having cancer caused me to focus 110%—otherwise I probably would have given only 99%."

Take a good look at your procrastinating behavior. What do you get as a result of this procrastinating? If your answer is action, then now become aware that you can get your action in a variety of different ways. You don't have to use procrastination to get it. What would bring more action into your life? Do you have the sense that your daily life is just a bit too safe? What would stir things up for you?

Get more action in your life and you won't need to procrastinate to get it.

**"I like to set difficult deadlines for myself.
I believe that the ultimate inspiration is the deadline."**
—Nolan Bushnell

If you're getting weary of too much "inspiration" because of your own behavior, you now have a choice.

What the Action Junkie Procrastinator gets:
1. Increased feeling of importance.
2. Intense focus.
3. Increased pressure and pace.

The prescription for the Action Junkie Procrastinator is: get more action in your life.

THE REBELLIOUS PROCRASTINATOR

"I procrastinate because I don't want to do it! It's that simple! I just don't want to! Nothing too complicated about that!"

Then make a decision to not do it. Decide not to clean the garage. Decide not to pay your taxes. Decide not to take your car in for an oil change.

If, however, it was your decision that these things be done and you're still not doing it out of some sort of inner rebellion, then you, too, are in good company. America was created and founded by people exactly like you! Procrastination is a way of reliving the '60's and saying, "You can't make me." We used to get a lot of attention for this kind of behavior. Capture the university president's office and smoke cigars at his desk. Drop a daisy down the barrel of a National Guardsman's M-16 rifle. "Hell, no, we won't go!" was the response to everything from going to war to going to the bathroom. We are all rebellious 2-year olds.

By using procrastination to resist anything (self-imposed or external), you may be asserting what little control you may feel you still have in your life.

When you get into a car and the dashboard lights up a notice that reads, "Fasten seat belt," do you have an internal reaction of resistance to that? Are parking meters just little metal authority figures to you? When you get an overdue notice in the mail are you just a little bit gleeful?

"Ben and I had been married for three years when our refrigerator broke down," Rachel explained. "That doesn't sound like such a big deal. It's just that Ben said that he would take care of it. When he says that, two things are implied: 1) I can't mention it to him because I'll sound like a nag, 2) I can't take over the job myself or I'll make him look bad. Guess how long we lived with a broken refrigerator? *Three months!* Guess how much it cost to finally have it fixed? $11! Ben's procrastination is driving me crazy! It gets to the point that I feel like I'm the enemy. I'm not the enemy—I'm his wife!"

The amount of irritation generated by the Rebellious Procrastinator cannot be calculated. The stakes are anything from refrigeration all the way up to large architectural projects and everything in between. Spousal play is very popular but bosses can play it with employees and employees use it on their bosses. The message is: "I don't have to and you can't make me."

What do you get from your procrastinating? If you answered "rebellion," then you can begin to cure yourself in the following ways:

1. There is remarkable freedom that comes from deciding NOT to do something. Only put things on your to-do list that you really want to do.

2. Say, "No, I don't want to do that," to requests that you have no intention of honoring. Delegate when appropriate. Let go of any of those refrigerator obligations.

3 Develop honesty muscles. If you're using procrastination to get fired or be asked for a divorce, just cut to the chase and end it.

4. Recognize that you have 2-year old tendencies and make sure this Inner Brat has other toys and other means of expression. Honor your desire to rebel by putting it to work for you (review suggestions above).

**"Outlaw or statesman...'tis a fine line
in a rebellious nature."**
—T. Duncan

What the Rebellious Procrastinator gets:
1. Manipulation of other people.
2. Temporary control.
3. Opportunity to flex "brat" muscles.
4. Chance to punish others.

The prescription for the Rebellious Procrastinator is: rebel! Write letters to Congress and to the "Letters to the

Editor" section of your newspaper and your favorite magazines. Attend neighborhood association meetings and back causes you believe in. Get involved with politics and run for office yourself. Start an underground newspaper or host a web site for your ideas. Put your view on a lawn sign and post it in your front yard. Do any productive rebellious thing that you can think of! Let that fiery inner patriot act! Then you won't have to use procrastination as the passive-aggressive alternative.

THE PERFECTIONIST PROCRASTINATOR

Mediocrity means "the quality or state of being normal." But the word "mediocrity" has received a lot of bad press and now nobody wants to be mediocre. We're all supposed to be "excellent" instead. And we know that we're not supposed to start a task until we can do it perfectly. The inarguable fact is that this is a ludicrous expectation.

"A job not done is imperfect."
—Anonymous

The Perfectionist Procrastinator may "put things on the back burner" until such time that the thoughts have incubated sufficiently. Artists and engineers use this technique and have good results with it. Albert Einstein would give his mind a task and then literally sleep on it then awaken with the solution. Unfortunately some of us have things that have been sitting on the back burner for so long that they've grown mold.

Procrastination protects the perfectionist. Procrastination allows us to believe that our ability is *greater than our performance*. What you see is not necessarily what we can do. It'll be great once we finally do it. But if we don't do it, we're safe for another day, safe from anyone measuring (and the person with the measurement may be ourselves). We can maintain a self-image of competence if we never actually get on stage to perform.

I'll bet you thought that a perfectionist is a person who goes around doing things, like fluffing up the pillows on the couch, correcting grammar, compulsively removing invisible lint from lapels, polishing their cars and balancing their checkbooks. The truth is that the perfectionist is not doing very much. They are saying things like:

"There's a right answer and I have to find it."

"More research and then I'll write it."

"It has to be perfect."

"I'll wait until I can do it perfectly."

When I was ten years old, sitting on my Aunt Grace's piano bench, I was frozen with indecision about the next note to play. Eighty-eight black and white keys presented themselves to me and they loomed so large, I felt like I was standing in front of Hoover Dam. My curled fingers were poised above the keys. I was confirming and reconfirming in my mind the right key to touch. My talented aunt sat next to me waiting, waiting for the next note to be played. Nothing came.

Finally in great desperation she said, "Do anything! Even if it's wrong!"

I learned a valuable lesson about procrastination that day. The silence of that piano was worse than anything...*anything!* I had been the victim of Analysis Paralysis. If it has to be done perfectly then, of course, you will freeze in front of the Piano Keys of Life.

A couple of decades passed and my daughter sent me an article that she wanted to submit to her college newspaper. I read the article and thought it was funny; I laughed at all the appropriate times. She asked for my opinion and I told her how much I enjoyed the article. One month later, I asked her about the article. She hadn't sent it in. My response was, "What? That was a good article!" Her predictable reaction was, "I just didn't know if it was good enough."

"Okay, here it is," I thought to myself. "You're looking right at the perfectionist procrastinator at work. What are you going to say next?"

My daughter was still shrugging her shoulders when I said, "You know what will probably happen if you submit that article? The newspaper staff will probably hold their noses and write red notes all over it and then send it to the journalism department. The head journalism prof will have copies made and passed around to all the classes as an example of lousy writing. They'll use your article as a standard of truly bad writing for years to come. It may even be reprinted in journalism textbooks as an example of what *not* to do. You'll be famous as the tackiest writer ever to hit a college campus and people will laugh and point at you on the street. You won't know how to handle such attention. You'll be a complete embarrassment to the whole family."

My daughter laughed and we dropped the subject. One month later I received a thank you note in the mail from my daughter with a recent issue of the university newspaper. The published article appeared on page 4 virtually unedited.

"There is nothing in this world worth doing that isn't going to scare you."
—Barbara Sher

The perfectionist has a sense of doom without ever answering the question, "What if I give it my all and it fails?" Chances are, the worst that would happen is not the worst thing that has ever happened to you! We think that if we give something our "all" and it is rejected that we won't be able to handle it. But when faced with the possibility that it really could be royally rejected, it is manageable. Could you handle it if it were rejected? Well, yeah. Would this rejection be the worst thing that has ever happened to you? Well, no.

Procrastination may be robbing you of your potential. Is it time for you to steal it back?

Perfectionists expect a lot from themselves. We hear things like, "Practice makes perfect." A perfectionist does not allow themselves the "practice" part.

"You can't hit 'em if you don't swing at 'em."
—Babe Ruth

What the Perfectionist Procrastinator gets:
1. Protection from criticism.

2. Security of a "well-thought out" plan.
3. Never having to say you're sorry.

The prescription for the Perfectionist Procrastinator: do it imperfectly. Practice looking ridiculous until it becomes second nature. Make a complete fool of yourself once a week. Ask yourself some questions:

1. Do I have enough information for this task? Will I *ever* have as much information as I'd like to have?
2. If I had a gun held to my head and I had to come up with a solution right now this minute, what would it be?
3. What would the perfect time frame be for this?
4. What is the worst that could happen if I act?
5. Has anyone ever survived such humiliation?
6. Is this the worst thing that has ever happened to me?
7. What is the *one thing* I could do *right now* to get me closer to completion?

(See Chapter 6.)

THE FEELING GOOD PROCRASTINATOR

"If it feels good, do it." That was a popular philosophy in the '60's and became almost a mantra in the '80's. The flip side of that must be: "If it doesn't feel good, don't do it." The Feeling Good Procrastinator feels a moral obligation to only do what feels good. It's almost a reverse of the Puritan's work ethic.

"I have avoided tasks that would take me outside my comfort zone," a fan named Dave wrote to me. "It is not possible to be successful in sales without being outside of your comfort zone most of the time. Weekends were my worst. I worked hard all week and I used to feel that my weekends had to be used for leisure—*no matter what!* I had an obligation to myself to goof off even when there were things that I really wanted to do. Part of me didn't want to turn into a high performance workaholic. And part of me wanted to get things done. I heard the advertising slogan 'You deserve a break today' and I took that literally.

"Then I heard your one line for the Feeling Good Procrastinator and it has changed my attitude, my self-talk and my discipline. My family and co-workers have noticed the change. I actually feel more comfortable with my life. It is enjoyable to get things done and it's all right for me not to like the chore, just to do it. Keep telling people that one great line because it is the thing that has made all the difference to me."

That one line is: **"You don't have to like it, you just have to do it."**

Got kids that hate their homework? Stop trying to convince them that they will become good people if they do their homework or that they'll get into a better college or be able to earn more money...some day. Instead just tell them, you don't have to like it, you just have to do it. They will be amazed at your wisdom and understanding!

We have bought into the idea that we have to have a good attitude or feel positively about something before we can act on it.

If I thought that I had to feel good about calories and carbohydrates and my insatiable appetite, I never would have lost 100 pounds.

When I finally let myself off that hook, I found that I could actually get things accomplished! Like Dave, I no longer have to talk myself into feeling good about a task. That is not required. All that is required is the action.

The Feeling Good Procrastinator is also the person who accepts an assignment they don't want, then puts it off rather than saying "no" in the first place. Saying "no" would make them feel bad. They think that saying "no" will make you feel bad. And they want to Feel Good, remember? Their message to you may be "don't rely on me." The message they may mean is, "Go away and leave me alone."

Any committee chairperson will say: "I want people who will accept an assignment and do it. I would prefer that someone not take on a task than to say they'll do it and then not get it done."

What the Feeling Good Procrastinator gets:
1. The sense that they are leading the "good life" because they only do what feels good.
2. The appearance of being a nice person because they don't say "no."
3. The illusion of personal freedom.

The prescription for the Feeling Good Procrastinator is: stop trying to feel good all the time. Repeat the phrase: YOU DON'T HAVE TO LIKE IT, YOU JUST HAVE TO DO IT. Say "no" when you can to things that you truly don't want to do. Let yourself do those things that you'd like to have done that are *less than wonderful* to do. Pamper yourself while you're doing the odious task (enjoy a cup of hot chocolate, sugar free of course, while you're working on your taxes, listen to your favorite music while you wax the car). Plan a reward for completing the task (finished those telephone cold calls? Take yourself out for lunch.)

SUMMARY:

If people stopped procrastinating, they would lose an effective way of dealing with situations. There are more creative solutions, however. Procrastination is a message from a part of you that wants something. Give yourself what the procrastination is giving you and you won't have to procrastinate to get it.

Instead of saying, "I don't have time," say, "It's just not a big enough priority for me right now." Because that would be the truth. Once you make a commitment to your own higher need, you've taken responsibility for your choice. When it becomes important to you, the time will miraculously be there.

Chapter 10
The Career Sabotage and Fear of Success

**"It's frightening to be successful
beyond your own imagination."**
—Tom Rusk

"Some people just beg to be fired," writes Jacqueline Kramer in *Today's Careers*. "They complain about being overworked yet never seem to complete a project. They talk back when they aren't busy complaining. Their bosses attempt to discuss their problems with them to little avail. When the axe falls, no one is surprised except the employee in question. In most cases, this sabotage happens unconsciously."

Who in their right mind would sabotage their work? To an outside observer this behavior brings only negative consequences—criticism, probation or even firing. For the person doing it, however, that "negative" consequence might be exactly what they're after.

When I had a perfectly good employee turn rotten (see Jim's story in Chapter 3) I did not have the concept that someone would actually try to get fired. I'd never heard of anything like that before. The idea was completely new to me and such a shock. (Remember it's hard to see the picture when you're part of the frame.) Once I stood in the line of sight of this different perspective, however, it became quite clear. (He's a #7 under "What's the benefit section," this chapter.)

Anxiety can blur your mind to consequences and cause you to make poor choices. Yet self-sabotage is just as likely to strike when things are going well. Example: After winning a prestigious law award, a prominent California attorney was caught stealing rulers and small items from judges' chambers.

Why?

Imagine a large sheet of plexiglass is floating in front of you. On that glass is an image that you hold of yourself. Position this glass over the real you. If there is enough of a match, you're fine. If the self-image doesn't match up to the accomplishments or position in life, however, sabotage might be in order.

Quick check: Are you sabotaging your work?
1. It's repeated.
   You have repeatedly been fired. You have repeatedly selected an employer and then discovered something wrong (with them) and left. You have *repeatedly* selected different careers, gotten yourself an education in that field, tried the field and then left it. You have *repeatedly* come close to a promotion or a contract and by some strange coincidence it has eluded you. Check your daily "to-do" list. Do you have the same list of things to do every day for more than three days? It should be more obvious that you don't want this list.
2. It's stupid. There's no getting around it, what you did was nuts and nobody in their right mind would have tried it.

Example: There's the case of former senator Gary Hart, whose alleged affair with an actress cost him a shot at the White House. Did he unconsciously instigate destroying his campaign? Or was he simply caught? Psychologists following the story say Hart was so reckless—at one point even daring the media to tail him—that he must have *wanted* to get caught. And that makes it self-sabotage. A test for self-sabotage is the stupidity factor: "If the No. 1 comment everybody makes about the behavior is that it was really dumb, it probably indicates self-sabotage."

Why do so many public figures self-destruct once they have fame and fortune?

It's too easy to say "Well, they felt they didn't deserve it, so they engineered their own downfall." Proponents of self-esteem are quick to put their theories on famous political foot-shooters. However, the higher need (accomplished by the sabotage) may be more elusive, more mysterious. This section covers: four ways we sabotage our work, seven benefits of the work sabotage and what you can do about a career sabotage.

> **"I predict that cloning will not become popular.
> Too many people already find it difficult
> to live with themselves."**
> —Jeanne Dixon

Have you or are you sabotaging your work life? How would you know? Roughly 90% of solving self-sabotage is recognizing it's you that's sabotaging. The remaining 10% is the grit required to knock it off.

4 Ways We Sabotage Our Work

1. Divide.

Hold down a full time job, sign up for college courses, volunteer to teach skiing and now go out and buy a dog. Individually these are all great activities. Collectively one has to wonder—are you nuts? When you're late for work because the ski bus didn't get you home til 2 A.M. and the dog eats your furniture out of loneliness and you miss three class lectures, even your friends lose sympathy for you.

When you're divided there is no rest; you're always trying to satisfy too many factions inside you. This has been labeled "personal terrorism."

A college dean, also a devoted soccer coach, had an active hobby of collecting train memorabilia and riding trains. She put in at least ten hours a week with the Girl Scouts. When I asked a student how the dean could possible do all these things, the student replied, "You haven't met her husband." The dean was honored and decorated by the Scouts, her fellow hobbyists and her college. It is almost impossible to break out of this lifestyle when you receive a lot of "attaboys" for your devotion. The dean was a virtual stranger in her own home; her excessive activities were a clear message.

> **"We're here to do something, not everything."**
> —Henry David Thoreau

A young man with a non-stop critical wife went to trucking school, graduated and hit the road all under the guise of increasing his take home pay. His long distance hauling took him all over the U.S. He stayed on the road until his inevitable divorce was final. It is interesting to note that when the papers were signed, he found local work.

Higher needs are met in interesting ways. We may use sabotage over finances to get attention, sabotage our weight for protection but we sabotage our work for an infinite number of benefits. Trying to serve two or more masters—a full time job and a full time interest—divides us and protects us from being great in either one.

"When you chase two rabbits, both escape."
—Zen quote

2. Flame Out.

This is a spontaneous combustion act that alters a career and/or relationship forever, the crash and burn in Dilbert Land, the flame out. You don't have to be an addict to engage in reckless behavior that sabotages your job, but it certainly helps if you want to flame out. Drug and alcohol abusers like Robert Downey, Jr. are classic flame outs. An even more powerful drug is the part of You that is after something different for you. That's where the real power is!

Examples: An executive earning a six figure income shoplifted a $9 item from a store without altering his brain chemistry yet! The employee who had his moonlighting clients leave work for him with the receptionist at his corporate job. The fighter pilot who told off his commanding officer after a few drinks at the officer's club. Obvious flame outs.

Without alcohol and drugs you've got a chance of having a successful career. But with it, it's just too much of a risk. Too many flame outs have been fueled by alcohol. Office Christmas parties are historically famous for lubricating people right into behavior that gets them fired.

A small town minister efficiently slaughtered both his job and his marriage by having an affair with the church choir director. Unable to muster the courage to make the changes he wanted, he chose the devastating route instead. Devastating to his religious community, to his wife but also his mistress who was jettisoned when his career transformation was complete.

The unfortunate thing about career sabotage is that, unlike the other forms of sabotage, other people are affected.

If your job depends on how some other worker does their job—and they are sabotaging—then they're not the only one with the problem, are they? No! This means you get to participate too! I don't like being an innocent bystander to someone else's sabotage. I want to be able to recognize self-sabotaging behavior in others so I can *get out of the way!*

Before it happens the Flame Out self-sabotage can be the most difficult one to spot. There may be no gradual indication of the fiery end approaching. It just sort of happens. Subconsciously we know what will bring a swift conclusion to our employment. You can steal something, you can flagrantly harass the wrong person, you can send an angry memo full of 4-letter words or you can simply go A.W.O.L. If you have fantasies about flame out behavior, examine the benefits you'll derive. Then make changes with conscious awareness, in short, do it with some class. Own up to the changes you want to make and take responsibility without sabotaging.

Part of the appeal of the flame out is the resulting humiliation at having done such a stupid thing. Understand that some people want that humiliation. Do you suspect that you do?

3. Martyr.

The classic delusion of all time is the martyr. It would be fine if a person who is a martyr would just sacrifice and leave it at that. But they don't. They extract their payment of sympathy with whining or by passively expressing resentment in a variety of ways. If they'd just stay up on their crosses and bleed it might not be so bad. Unfortunately most martyrs like an audience. The martyr is the person who terrorizes themselves by constantly letting other people's feelings—real or imagined—come first.

Examples: The person who can't make it to the job interview because of perceived family obligations. The person who won't further their work skills by taking a day long seminar or night course because they are so needed elsewhere. The writer who won't submit their screenplay because success would scare their spousal unit too much. The employee who won't retire and try a second career because "they need me down there." The volunteer who generously gives of their time so much that there is no time left for anything else. The employee who repeatedly sacrifices a promotion because of _____ (fill in the blank).

Secretly, a martyr resents obligations they think they have to family, friends, spouse and employer. Some people feel selfish when they concentrate on themselves or their careers. Ambitious? Ambition is only OK for Olympic athletes and super stars but not us. That's how we were raised. Your life, however, is no less important than an athlete's. Your career deserves your attention.

When it comes to taking time for themselves—for better health or enhancing a career or investing in an art—most martyrs can't do it. They don't even allow themselves to dream. If you dream long enough or intensely enough, pretty soon you have to take responsibility for those dreams. Martyrs leave the responsibility to others.

**"I don't know the key to success
but the key to failure is trying to please everybody."**
—Bill Cosby

Every evening do you feel as if you've parceled out portions of your day to everyone else? Is this a temporary challenge or has it become your lifestyle?

4. Broken Record.

A relative of mine called from Cancun aglow with descriptions of his new dream job. He'd left his employment with a dive shop in Hawaii for the equally clear and beautiful waters of the posh resorts in Mexico. The cost of living was better, he gushed and not only was he teaching diving every day but he was earning even more money by using his underwater camera to take keepsake photos of diving tourists. When I asked about the management and the longevity of his new employer, these were glossed over. He continued to rave about the weather, the fabulous hotels full of turistas lining the pier waiting to give their money to the dive school.

It sounded like heaven except for one little thing. I'd heard it all before. The boss who arrived in his Mercedes, the promises of shared profits, the endless stream of happy paying customers. Sure enough. Before a year was up, the Cancun dive shop was run by morons, the clients were pesky spoiled jerks and my relative had been promised even greater rewards in the Florida Keys, so he was headed there.

When he called from Big Pine Key I was tempted to record his phone call. So enthusiastic, so positive! And oddly similar to Hawaii and Cancun and a half dozen other great opportunities that mysteriously turned bad. The pattern became so predictable that I considered guessing a date of when this new idyllic situation would also turn sour. How long would it take the successful Florida boss to turn into the same kind of moron who ran the Cancun operation? How long would it take for this wonderful dive shop to become like the hellhole in Hawaii? Only a matter of time.

This is the Broken Record Syndrome. It causes the same song lyric to play over and over and over again. After awhile people lose interest in hearing about the great new job and how wonderful it's going to be. And they're definitely not interested when this job is being trashed.

My relative refuses to ask the important questions when researching a job. Like, how long have you been in business? He gets very loyal, very fast and then resents it when he is over-worked and unappreciated. He never bothers to ask about performance reviews or criteria, length of service of other employees, the company's long range plans, their customer service policy, in short, the questions you'd like to know before you devote your time (your life!) to this outfit.

When people get tired of the chaos and upheaval caused by this type of career sabotage, they start asking the important questions. A person who constantly wants to take center stage in a drama is the person who finds the employment merry-go-round. All the carousel horses are the same, they're just painted different colors. The music is the same song and when the ride stops you haven't advanced to anywhere. You've had a fun ride, full of ups and downs, that's for sure.

Ask yourself, have I heard myself complain about these same things before? Have all my supervisors been jerks? Whose fault is that? You have to own *some* responsibility for choosing those jerks, don't you? Do you have a knack for picking companies that go bankrupt? What sort of attention are you getting for this act? Does mom ring her hands every time you leave one job for another? Do you feel somehow strangely vindicated when you give notice? What is it about the whole drama that you find so enticing?

Seven Benefits (the Why's) of Career Sabotage

1. Get back what's comfortable (and known)

The engineering firm was doing well. Growing every year, they landed more projects and hired more people. The three original partners were still running things. Walls were being knocked out in their building to accommodate more staff, more engineers, some planners and support staff. Projections for their future went nothing but up.

One day I met with one of the partners about some projects. He looked particularly haggard. He seemed to have trouble concentrating and I asked him, "Anything the matter?" He stared off down the long hall outside his office and he said, "You know, I was walking down the hallway this morning and I crossed paths with someone I didn't even know." I wasn't sure what the partner was talking about. "Here's an employee of this company and I didn't even know his name," he went on. "I can remember when all this company was, was three engineers and three draftsmen." His voice was sad.

That seemingly insignificant comment took on new meaning for me as I watched this engineering firm gradually start to shrink. They merged with another firm but continued to downsize. Their sterling reputation never faltered, fortunately, but they just got smaller and smaller.

I came to understand that the discomfort that this engineering partner felt was stronger than the need for growth. We tend to want what is familiar. If we act or are treated in unfamiliar ways—even if it's better—we become increasingly uncomfortable and we consciously or unconsciously act to bring ourselves back to what's comfortable.

One smart entrepreneur said, "I will not make this company into the job that I left behind." She kept her successful company mid-sized rather than recreate the corporate job that she had worked so hard to leave.

A successful jewelry artist was interviewed for a business segment on the news and asked if he was going to now have his designs mass produced overseas. He was horrified by the question. "I do this for the joy of working with my hands. Why would I turn this into a management function?"

Many of us who travel to Europe like to get off the beaten path and stay in unusual inns and little hostels. We may shudder at the idea of eating at the McDonald's in Paris or staying at the Holiday Inn in London. Why on earth would anyone travel to fabulous Europe and go to such Americanized places? After putting up with some pretty odd sleeping quarters, however, I can see why people would chose an American franchise. It's familiar. After several weeks of language differences, foreign money exchange, incomprehensible food choices and horsing around with the phone and postal system (not to mention 50 ways to flush a toilet), I can see why someone would chose to be around something a bit familiar. It is stressful to be so far outside your comfort zone for an extended period of time. It might begin to wear on you after awhile.

It may be under the guise of the Peter Principle (rising to your level of incompetence), some people will sabotage their careers until they are safely back within their comfort zones.

2. Parental messages.

"Don't get above your raisin'..."

I asked Myra to "become her mother" and talk about Myra. What came next was an insightful conversation about competition. Myra had no conscious awareness that her mother felt upstaged by her talented daughter until Myra did this exercise. If you "became your" mother or father for a few minutes, what would you have to say about your kid (you)? I promise that if you take 5 minutes and do this exercise it will bring you surprises. Reach for a pen now and write it out.

Do it.

Many of us would find it difficult to show up at the family reunion and be very different from the other relatives. We want to succeed...just not too much.

Joe Dubay, career counselor extraodinaire, believes some parents send a subtle warning to children "not to do better than they have, and this message stays embedded in their children's psyches throughout their adult life." This, in turn, often leads adults to inadvertently hurt themselves career-wise.

"Success in life means not becoming like your parents."
—Louise Bowie

3. "This is a test."

It's a popular old theme: the prince or the princess who leaves the castle in a disguise to find "true love," the person who will love them rather than their royal position. Everyone seems to know that when you have trouble in life, you'll "find out who your friends are."

If you're uncomfortable with your fame and fortune, it could account for your self-destructive behavior. "I can't possibly be this perfect," you may be saying to yourself and to people who know you. After teaching my teamwork seminar a successful manager stepped up to me and said, "I've been able to accomplish anything I've set out to do, except that." He pointed to the "before" photograph of me weighing over 200 pounds. "That makes you human then, doesn't it?" I said. Sometimes we've worked so hard to get everything going the right way for us that we have to have one area that stumps us. We need to have non-success somewhere in our lives. Anyone who gets the feeling that things are just becoming too perfect is a prime candidate for career sabotage.

"Unsure whether they're admired for their true selves or just their status and money," says one psychiatrist, "some *have to fail* to find out who their real friends are."

4. The Fun is in the Clean Up or I Wonder If I Can Get Away With This...

Somewhere on the campaign trail President Bill Clinton picked up the moniker of the Come Back Kid. He seemed to be able to "come back" from any kind of scandal no matter how sordid. In 1999 this was tested at the expense of a country nauseated (yet still fascinated) by the news coverage.

Anytime you have the image of yourself as the Come Back Kid, what do you have to do? You have to come back from something, right? The press was quick to point out that Clinton and his spousal unit are at their best when the mud starts to fly. The fun, for some people, is in cleaning up and holding their heads high under mountains of wet flying dirt. "Getting caught is the mother of invention," writes Robert Byrne.

"Life is a daring adventure...or it is nothing."
—Helen Keller

Everyone admires Helen Keller; there is no doubt she was an exceptional person. If they don't know that Helen Keller said the above quote, we all know from Indiana Jones movies that we're supposed to be having daring adventures. When my life seemed to be one daring adventure after another with no time for anything else, I began to see how this quote had been affecting me. Part of me longed for a few days of no daring adventures.

I had felt a moral obligation to accept any daring adventure (especially if it involved travel) because to do otherwise Life would be ordinary and dull. I wouldn't be living my life to its fullest if I wasn't off doing daring adventures. Well, nuts to that. It really is OK to have things be calm, regular and peaceful from time to time. That "Life is a daring adventure" stuff can be an open invitation to sabotage your career. This is prevalent enough that I think it could actually be considered a syndrome—the person who has to keep themselves constantly on the edge to keep motivated because they took Helen Keller a little too seriously.

One business owner explained: "I don't need extreme sports. I have my business for all the terror I'll ever need."

Winners do not look for excitement *just* to break rules or beat the system.

5. "This can't last."

The other shoe is about to drop. You can just sense it coming.

In a misguided attempt to be in control, some people shoot themselves in the foot before fate or someone else does it for them.

For added drama, some mix romance with a little business. There's the executive who combined unhappiness at work (running his relative's business) and unhappiness at home by having an affair with his secretary. That wasn't enough sabotage evidently because the executive was arrested at a shopping mall for indecent exposure. At some unconscious level he was asking to be destroyed.

"Into every life a little rain must fall."
—old adage

And by golly, if the rain doesn't show up, we'll find a way to rain on our own parades.

A subset of this self-sabotage phenomenon is the person who feels that if you win something, you have to lose something else. If you win a promotion, you have to now have a punishment: a car accident, a weight gain, a marital hassle.

6. Deserving it.

"No good deed goes unpunished."
—Clare Boothe Luce

Thanks a bunch, Clare, like we needed this one.

Bob was working very hard to make his carpentry business work. He also paid close attention to his family life and his own health. He could never seem to get all the balls in the air, however and one evening he discovered why. When a group of friends were discussing who deserved to win the lottery, Bob suddenly became aware that he didn't feel as if he deserved success in Life. Why not? Bob's twin brother had committed suicide when the boys were teenagers. Bob had somehow given himself the idea that if his brother had been denied a life that Bob, too, should be denied a life. He was constantly having to struggle for his success at every level—his business, his family and his health because part of him was trying to destroy it all. He was always two steps forward, one and a half steps back.

This "deserving it" thing is tough. And even the tough have a tough time with it. Most remarkable is the story of Lewis Puller Jr., the decorated Marine who lost one third of his body in Vietnam to a booby trap and went on to write his Pulitzer Prize-winning autobiography, *Fortunate Son.* Puller questioned whether he was worthy of the admiration that his book had brought. "He became massively depressed," said Sen. Bob Kerrey, who had spent months in a hospital ward with Puller. At the age of 48, Puller shot and killed himself.

Do you deserve the success that you have?

If you went for a walk this afternoon and found a $20 bill blowing in the street, would you ask yourself if you deserve to have it? No! You'd pick it up and say to yourself, wow!

If it helps to blame your success on luck, then do that. Just claim it and get on with your life.

7. Lack of self-knowledge.

If you lack the ability to identify what you want, you're in the front row for sabotaging your career. Jim didn't know that he wanted to move back to Seattle and subconsciously worked to get himself fired.

Much of the self-handicapping behavior that one job recruiter has seen falls into this category. "One of the biggest problems is people who don't know what they want to do. They just want a job," she says. "This attitude is reflected in resumes with mismatched objective statements or in inappropriate interview behavior."

"People may dress inappropriately for an interview, fail to ask questions and do not make frequent eye contact because, subconsciously, they don't want the job or believe they aren't skilled enough for the position," writes Jacqueline Kramer in *Today's Careers*. She goes on to list basic traits that are common in career self-sabotage:

- Blaming others for your troubles
- Believing that failure is imminent
- Counting on luck rather than skill or planning
- Failing to learn from past mistakes
- Refusing to be flexible
- Being unable to make decisions
- Being unable to delegate tasks
- Feeling overly cautious

"People come to life-transitional points," says Joe Dubay, "and there's a sense of acting out and sabotaging oneself rather than doing the inner work and the inner reflection needed to deal with those transitions."

A typical response by this type of self-saboteur is, "I want something (career-wise) that I shouldn't want."

What You Can Do About Career Sabotage

1. Get thee to a career counselor.

Find a good one (references) and go! It will be money well invested. If you've become a real pain in the neck as an employee, you may even get your company to pay for it. Since career sabotage affects your family and your current work place, you'll be doing everybody a favor. Only you can check why you are hurting your career.

2. Get Barbara Sher's *Wishcraft: How To Get What You Really Want.*

The first half of this book is figuring out what you want which for some of us hasn't been easy. (Most of us don't just wake up when we're five years old and *know* that we want to be dentists. Just doesn't work that way.) The second half of the book is schemes on how to get there (wherever your "there" is). This is not a book that you read, it's a book that you do. There are plenty of insightful exercises and avenues for creativity. The examples of radical career transitions are inspiring.

Barbara Sher has heard many people claim that they wanted to live passionately, but that they were stuck because they didn't know what would truly keep their full attention. "Everyone is unconsciously engaged in a internal battle for control of direction," says Sher. "Their lives are full of clues, they just don't know how to look for them. We can't go forward if we don't know what's holding us back."

There is an internal part of You who knows exactly what that is—this part has a higher need for you, a Very Good Reason. *Wishcraft* will be embraced by this part of you. *Wishcraft* is a practical, common sense strategy that lets you have "off" days, a lousy attitude and have all the fear and laziness that you want. Barbara Sher says she's never heard a dream she thought was frivolous.

One last note...

If you go for something and it doesn't "take"—a job interview, a new client, a stalled business enterprise—just before you start feeling down, I want you to remember the Rialto Bridge in Venice. Get a picture of this bridge and post it in your work space. Because Michelangelo *lost the contract to design this bridge.* Can you believe it? Someone turned down Michelangelo? Descendants of the selection committee for the

Rialto Bridge exist today. They are everywhere; you may have delivered a proposal to them just this morning. Yes, they got their bridge and yes, it is distinctive...but *Michelangelo?!*

Michelangelo probably didn't lose much sleep over that little deal judging from his output since that rejection. Take a lesson from this master.

"Work is love made visible."
—Kahlil Gibran

Chapter 11
The Coupling Sabotage

**"We are overrun by men and women pioneering
ways of finding the
wrong partners and losing the right ones."**
—Roy Rivenburg

The remarkable thing about human beings is: they get what they want even when they don't know what that is.

You will work like crazy to get the weight off, even submit to having jaws wired and stomachs stapled, when there's really a powerful part that wants the weight on.

You will pinch pennies and squander dollars. If you've been struggling with finances for more than five years, consider the concept that part of you has a higher need to be strapped for money.

You will profess to want a clean garage, a novel written and taxes paid on time when actions tell us just the opposite. If you've battled procrastination, imagine that someone inside you has a higher need for putting things off for you.

You say you want a "lasting relationship" when marriages barely outlast milk.

If you've been a participant in multiple relationships, consider the audacious idea that you *don't really want one.*

American advertising tells you that you are looking for one. Your religious community prays to deliver you one. Your mother waits for a miracle to happen for you: the "right" person. Myths and fairy tales prime you to expect one. Television and movies strike right at the heart of your heart that is just a half a heart until you find the other half. Song lyrics ("You're nobody til somebody loves you"), cruise ships, personal ads, dating services and all your friends just know that it's only a matter of time. In fact, it appears that you're a tad weird if you aren't:

- in a romantic relationship
- actively looking for a romantic relationship
- licking your wounds (temporarily) over a romantic relationship (and you'll be back in the game soon)

or

- waiting for him or her to show up

Wasn't there just the tiniest sense of relief inside you when that last relationship ended? No matter how shocked you may have been or how devastated—admit it, wasn't there a voice inside you that said, "Thank God that's over."

A recent study reports that people solve complex problems better in the presence of their dogs than they do when they are alone. And they perform better alone than they do in the presence of their spouses. When I share the details of this study with audiences they always guess under which circumstances people do their best and they always know that the study subjects with spouses did their worst. The audience *never fails* to guess correctly! How do they know?

I think it's because they already know that men and women have limited use for each other's company. There, it's been said.

"It has only been recently that men and women have had to start talking to each other," writes Joe Tanenbaum in *Male and Female Realities.* "Up until now, it hasn't been necessary. We've begun to ask, 'Would you like to sit and talk?'—only to discover that we can't. My observations have led me to the opinion that men and women are not designed to be around each other all the time."

Imagine: You are a biologist studying two sets of mammals. After careful observation you have concluded that the following differences exist between these two mammal groups:

- muscle and skeletal structure is different
- brain size and brain chemistry is different
- internal organs—size and placement also different

- different metabolic rates
- different breathing and skin sensitivity
- radically different glands and hormones
- eyesight is different
- hearing and vocal cords are different
- flexibility and stamina are different
- immune systems are different
- one set of mammals is drawn to objects;
- the other is drawn to other mammals
- one set of mammals has less hair, bruises more easily
- the other mammals have 17% more muscle
- the skull shapes are different
- they respond differently to heat and light
- in one set of mammals 30% more die in the first 3 months of life

One would safely begin to conclude that these two sets of mammals are of a different species. Expectations for observations in behavior should be different for these two groups of mammals.

But they aren't: they're called human men and human women and our current societal structure expects them to pair off and live in the same pen together.

What gave us the idea that we should be coupled anyway?

> **"Marriage is the unsuccessful attempt to make something lasting out of an incident."**
> —Albert Einstein

And yet, our entire system of law and housing and entertainment is geared to the obsession of pairing. We no longer need to concern ourselves with carrying on our life form. We're hardly nearing extinction. Most critters naturally cut back when they've overstocked the woods, streams and plains with their species. It's more than a biological imperative. Of all the compulsions possible, the energy put into the compulsion to pair up is beyond comprehension. It defies sanity. "Love," wrote Ortega y Gasset, "is transitory imbecility." (And you thought *I* was radical!)

"In measuring biological differences between men and women," writes Joe Tanenbaum, "the human male has more in common with some other species, particularly apes, than with human females."

**"Men and women. Women and men.
It will never work."**
—Erica Jong

A new and healthy living style needs to be introduced to a populace made sick with sabotage.

People are forever trying to kill themselves with drugs, food, cigarettes. Those are fairly obvious. Ones that aren't so obvious are: obliterating ourselves financially, screwing up careers and, of course, the ever-popular "let's ruin a relationship." This last one may be the *most* popular American pastime. At some point, however, some people get bored with being poor and pretty soon they have money. They get weary with job moves, tired of creating ways to buck the system and they find careers they like. When they get bored with the emotional chaos brought on by relationship wars, they get exhausted with the FIGHT. And they give up and start getting along or they discover a lifestyle that finally works for them.

The culture needs to accommodate a new preferred status: the Solitaire. It has only been in recent years that food packaging has acknowledged the person who eats alone. Housing designers and automobile designers can follow that lead.

The new lifestyle can be called "living as a solitaire." It is a preferred circumstance just as one would say, "I'm a dentist" is your preferred profession.

Does this sound radical to you? I hope so because conventional thinking isn't working.

I listened to a woman one evening say that her husband was away on business for two weeks and she was frightened. We assumed that she meant that she was afraid to be in her house by herself. "No," she said, "he's been gone only a few days and I really like being alone—I mean, I really, *really* like it..."

"I want to be terribly close
to someone who will leave me alone."
—Anonymous

Could it be that many of us are natural Solitaires and don't know it? Are we going to have to wait until ***How to Make a Success of Your Fifth Marriage*** shows up on the *New York Times* bestseller list before we get the message?

Is it remotely feasible that after a few marital detours that we settle into marriages and just finally shut up and live with it because we're too tired to fight any longer and not creative enough to discover an alternative? Do we just give up and stay married this time quietly admitting to ourselves that this one isn't that much different than the first one?

The drive to unite with another human being is, I think, stronger than any appetite we have. It is stronger than the longing for chocolate or the overwhelming aroma of fresh baked bread. If most entrepreneurs put as much energy and thought into their businesses, they'd all be successful and wealthy. Nothing can compare to the drive and the elation when we think we have found our "soul mates." And this time it's going to be different.

"The happiest of all lives is a busy solitude."
—Voltaire

Solitary women top the happiness charts. According to numerous research studies the unmarried woman is the happiest with her lot in life. More women would choose this lifestyle if:

(a) it were socially acceptable.

(b) they could afford it.

That last paragraph might give real pause for concern. How can I tell if I'm being chosen out of economic necessity? Perhaps the increase in sexual heat in the human male is there to override their ability to consider this possibility.

If you're happily coupled, that's great. Rare and great. Then this is not an issue for you. You may be in the 50% of the population that can tolerate coupling with minimal stress. But if you were happily coupled you probably wouldn't be reading this, unless you are trying to understand someone who isn't happily coupled. A percentage of the population truly is satisfied and even ecstatic with their living arrangements and choice of spouse or partner. A percentage.

Then there's the other percentage. Those are the people I want to address.

I'd like to suggest that "You're nobody til somebody loves you" can be interpreted to mean "You're nobody til somebody loves you and that somebody is inside you, not outside you."

Do you suspect that you may be a natural Solitaire? Read through this list of traits and see what fits.

Yes or No

_____ Interruptions are difficult for me. If I am interrupted while working or deep in thought, it seems to affect me more than others.

_____ I admire thinking and I enjoy thinking about things.

_____ It is a delicious treat to take myself out for coffee or for a meal by myself.

_____ My surroundings are radically different than they would be if I had created and decorated by myself.

_____ Even though I get along well with people, I suspect that I'm really a closet introvert.

_____ Someone has observed that I am not especially nurturing, spontaneous or sympathetic.

_____ I feel guilty for asking for alone time, or I've given up asking for it altogether.

_____ I fantasize about my spouse or partner's death and it doesn't scare me.

_____ I wish my partner would have an affair.

_____ I am not afraid to be alone.

_____ I relish being alone.

_____ I can't wait until I'm alone again.

_____ The best part of my day is my commute to and from home and office.

_____ People would be shocked if they knew how shy I really am.

_____ My initial reaction when I get a meeting notice is: "Oh, nuts, not another meeting!"

_____ More than once this week I have said to myself, "I could get so much done if people would just leave me alone."

_____ I love research and analysis.

_____ I'm 15 years behind in projects…and those are just my hobbies.

_____ Left to my own devices, I could solve most of my problems.

_____ I think and/or work better in silence.

_____ The lyrics to song, _People,_ have never made any sense to me.

_____ I like to figure out how things work.

_____ I prefer writing on paper that has lines.

_____ If all I had to contend with was _me,_ I'd have a fine life.

_____ I overeat around other people.

_____ I spend more money when I shop with another person.

_____ Traveling with another person is usually frustrating or impossible.

_____ I seem so different than everyone else, I must be eccentric.

_____ When I come home after a very exhausting day or long business trip, I am relieved when I discover that everybody else has gone to bed.

_____ Things that are big things to other people are simple things to me if I do them alone (e.i. grocery shopping).

_____ My life would be wonderful if I could just have 10 more minutes alone every day.

_____ I have my best ideas when I'm by myself.

_____ I enjoy a long drive or a long ride alone.

_____ I get great solutions to things when I'm in the shower.

_____ I'd rather take my brain out and play with it than do just about anything.

_____ I feel edgy around my spouse at times for no apparent reason and I have no idea why.

_____ When I imagine my perfect day and my perfect life I wake up alone.

_____ I'd pay the extra to not have to have "double occupancy" on a tour.

_____ I don't find it particularly difficult to live with me and can't imagine why anyone else would.

_____ I make sense to me.

_____ I am not interested in sharing my shaver.

_____ I enjoy finding things where I left them.

_____ I am organized and I am frustrated by people who aren't.

If you answered "yes" to 10 or more items, you may be a Solitaire who is strait jacketed in conventional thinking. If you also find yourself in and out of multiple relationships, examine the possibility the there is a part of You that knows full well that you are a natural Solitaire. You may overeat to stuff these feelings of frustration of living with someone. You may overspend to try to keep yourself happy when really only solitude will help. You may sabotage your relationship and have a list of grievances about your partner, not knowing that the real lover you long for is solitude.

A Solitaire may be someone who loves to think and play with possibilities. They need time and silence to mix divergent ideas and see patterns. Heaven to a Solitaire is being able to find things like scissors where they left them.

For half the population finding the family scissors is annoying but it's no big deal. For the part of the population that is _natural solitaire_ and in denial of it, finding the scissors becomes a bonafide stressor.

It is easier in our culture to admit that you're gay than it is to admit that what you really and truly want is to be left alone. "Coming out" has been a major ordeal for many homosexuals. They remember the date and they cringe to remember their feelings. This is nothing as radical as admitting to yourself and to the world that you don't crave the opposite sex and you don't crave your own sex either. What you really crave is a monogamous relationship with Yourself. Now *that's* deviant!

"One of the advantages of living alone is that you don't have to wake up in the arms of a loved one."
—Marion Smith

"I regard the 'compulsion to couple' as if everybody is rushing down an interstate freeway," a writer explained to me. "Everyone is speeding on the Relationship Highway and there are some people who are causing accidents with their bad driving. Some drivers are yelling typical things at them that you'd expect to hear like, 'Get off the road! Why don't you pull over until you learn how to drive?' It occurred to me that I was one of those poor drivers. I just didn't seem to be getting the hang of it and I was irritating the other drivers on the road. So I pulled over and parked. I thought I would just get out and walk for awhile but now I've walked far enough away from the freeway that I can see it for what it is and I don't want to go back. My old vehicle, Romance, is still parked and abandoned beside the road. I've been so happy ever since I grasped this perspective. There's nothing wrong with me. I just don't want to drive on that highway anymore. I see no reason for me to participate. It seems like the world is happier and I know that I am."

"I feel so much better now that I've had my dating gland removed."
—Anonymous

It can be awkward and almost impossible to ask a partner for more Alone time. The response is usually, "What's wrong?" We have the mistaken notion that something has to be "wrong" for us to be brave enough to ask for solitude. Since it is so difficult to say the words, "I just want to be alone" (only Garbo could pull it off with panache), one married couple hit on a brilliant solution. They both agreed that they wanted more Alone time and they both agreed that it was difficult to just ask for it. They also agreed that they could not read each other's minds and shouldn't be expected to. They created a visual sign between them that meant, "I'm alone now. Do not disturb." He would wear his old fishing hat whenever he wanted to be left alone and she would wear a red bandana around her neck.

Now he could sit and read his newspaper wearing his fishing hat and get through the entire paper uninterrupted. She could be out in the garden and if the phone rang and it was for her, he would look out the back window for her and her red bandana. If she was wearing it, he would take a message for her. If she wasn't wearing it, he would call to her. Great system.

A seminar speaker on a cruise ship enjoyed teaching on cruises but was annoyed by the constant interruptions by people on the ship after the lectures were over. He finally realized that he was counting on people to read his mind. Then he hit on a solution. He wore a red lapel ribbon which meant, "Stop, don't bother to talk to me now." Without the ribbon, he instructed his audiences, he was happy to engage in conversation.

A field manager for a housing construction company was a natural Solitaire. He was married and trying to do a good job at work. He got along well with people but the effort was taking its toll. The interruptions in his office and out on the job site bothered him to no end. He felt the stress so acutely that he thought he may have to leave his job. Things changed when he developed a visual sign for when he was focused and needed to be left alone. He put a playing card in the window of his office to alert the office staff that he didn't want to be disturbed and on the job site he wore a bright colored baseball cap.

People have absolutely no way of knowing if your brain is engaged in serious thought and now would be a bad time to interrupt you. They don't know that speaking to you is interrupting you. The technique of having a visual sign that indicates "Later, please" is a way for a natural Solitaire to make it in a world full of other people. If you've been counting on other people to read your mind, then knock it off. You are asking for frustration and you're doing them no favors. They would prefer to have your undivided attention and not have you overcoming the stress of the interruption just to listen to them. What visual cue would work for you?

"Conversation enriches the understanding but solitude is the school of genius."
—Edward Gibbon

"It wasn't until I hit 50 that my friends and relatives stopped trying to fix me up with someone," a utility executive said in an interview of Lone Stars. "They finally gave up after a half century. Some think I'm gay and that I have women friends as a cover. I love women. I just need more solitude than the average person and I *know* that."

Know thyself—it keeps coming back to that, doesn't it?

Why is it that when someone says, "I love you" the other one reaches for a packing box and furniture starts to move? Why do we follow "love" with "live with"? Where did we get the idea that if several hours a week with this person is fun, that more hours will produce more fun? That's like thinking if having one dog is fun, having a hundred dogs would be even more fun.

We do it because separately we can afford a $300 stereo system but together we can afford a $500 stereo system. In order to get the standard of living we want, requires two incomes and you're willing to bring home only one. Perhaps an adjustment in what we call our "standard of *living*" would be appropriate here. For a natural Solitaire accepting a cheaper stereo system has got to be more preferable than facing another day of cringing every time you hear, "Hi, honey, I'm home."

"It destroys one's nerves to be amiable every day to the same human being."
—Benjamin Disraeli

This automatic conclusion to live together—is this working for us? Divorce statistics would certainly indicate that our present system isn't working. Could we just take a nano second and consider a possible healthy alternative?

Rhonda Fleming and her husband live in two separate but neighboring condominiums. "I need my privacy and so does he," the actress explained.

When my daughter was a young teenager she would visit a friend of hers who lived about 20 blocks away. When I agreed to pick her up at her friend's house she told me how to drive there, adding, "Either the blue house or the white house on the corner." So which one, I asked confused. She answered, "Either one. The blue house is her mother's house and the white house is her father's house. We'll either be in one or the other." These two parents lived next door to each other and the kids had the run of both houses.

Who could afford such an arrangement? Our system of housing is totally skewed to our obsession to pair up.

Boundary issues. We can start relationships in cozy fireside restaurants but they end up at the meat counter at Safeway. Walks on the beach are traded in for walking the stray dog that the kids brought home and named before we could get them to stop. And we've been in the company of others for so long that we don't know *what* we want for ourselves anymore.

Totally unaware of this—remember you're probably the last person to know that you're self-sabotaging—the loving relationship begins to unravel. It's work. And then it's "who needs this irritation?" That develops into "Life is too short." Unable to extricate ourselves simply we switch to passive aggressive strategies or outright wicked acts of deception. Eventually we learn one of the "50 ways to leave your lover" and it is blessedly over. Everything but the paperwork. And why are you depressed? Because you're *supposed to be.* You'll look heartless if you spring back too soon. You go through a sort of grieving process. You tell your friends that you don't want to date and for once in your life you are connected to that part of you that has craved solitude for so, so long.

But when the gift of solitude finally becomes a reality, you don't know what to do with it. You literally do not know what to do with the Alone time. And none of your friends are Solitaires and you have no role models for how a Solitaire is supposed to act.

**"God made everything in six days...
but He had the advantage of working alone."**
—Unknown

There's a difference between being lonely and being alone. Being busy and being alone, we call being "alone." Being alone and being *bored* is called being "lonely." So the term lonely has more to do with activity and interest and being interesting people than with being *alone*. When we're bored and alone we label that "lonely." We also say that we can be lonely in a crowd. That just means that we're bored and disconnected with other people, but we're also disconnected with ourselves.

Time for the Inner Theatre. Use this method and you'll never be lonely again. A primary requirement in using the Inner Theatre Method is alone time. And the Inner Theatre Method is the cheapest and most effective way to solve self-sabotage issues and to truly know yourself.

How has your mania to be connected affected your life? How many events have you attended physically when your true self would have taken you elsewhere? How much of your life have you given to socializing when your preference was peace and quiet? Whose life is it anyway?

**"Sing and dance together and be joyous, but
let each one of you be alone."**
—Kahlil Gibran in *The Prophet*

Why do these beautiful, poignant words appear in so many chosen wedding vows and then people go off to drive each other crazy with joint checking accounts and bathroom familiarity? For two reasons:

(a) because it's our habit—we have not examined another possibility.

(b) because it's cheaper.

Not everyone is cut out to be a Solitaire. The drive to connect spiritually, emotionally and physically with another human being is probably the strongest drive we have and those who succeed are richly rewarded. What gums up the works are people who *think* they want a relationship and deep within themselves they don't. These are the saboteurs that attract and then repel, confusing and annoying those around them. Their wake of devastation is incalculable and involves children. They may be the last ones to recognize their sabotaging behavior. If you've been in five or more what *you'd* call serious relationships and/or marriages, you might want to examine the possibility that there is a part of you that doesn't want a partner. You may be a Solitaire and not know it. If you tried a period of living alone and it didn't "take" that doesn't mean that part of you doesn't still require Alone time.

> **"A system could not well have been devised more studiously hostile to human happiness than marriage."**
> —Percy Bysshe Shelley

We all have what I call an "S" Quotient, a craving for Solitude. We all need solitude like we need food, air and water. Some of us need just a little solitude and we're on our way able to tolerate being in close company for hours and days on end. And we see no magic to it. Then there are others of us who require a great deal of solitude and feel that when we don't get enough of it we'll soon be arming ourselves and committing anti-social acts. It may start as a mild general frustration with people and progress to overt curmudgeon brutality. Normal traffic offenses could cause an instant and vicious reaction. Some people are attempting to drive automobiles while they are saturated with being around people—they are at capacity like water-logged sponges that can't handle any more. But our culture still tells us that we're only normal when we're tickled pink to be rubbing elbows with our fellow humans and that we somehow *require* interaction with other members of the species.

This is nonsense. It's also painful for the Solitaire who has been ruled by this kind of thinking too long. We crave having an hour to ourselves. And since we won't give ourselves that treat, we give ourselves dessert instead. Or an expensive gift. Instead of time alone we give ourselves the booby prize of food and stuff.

This just puts the sabotage in a different pocket. Now we're overweight and over budget and still have the feeling that we've spent the day wearing a sandpaper suit because we haven't gotten what we really want: time alone. Writers and artists have to eventually admit that writing and painting and sculpting are not group activities. Are you being forced to move "to the rhythm of others"?

Both the need to be alone and the need to connect to others are to be balanced by your own individual *requirement.* I believe that the amount of solitude needed varies with the individual. But we all need *some.* "Without solitude we lose the important sense of being self-regulating individuals. There is no denying that many of our social and psychological 'diseases' are primarily disturbances in self-regulation," writes Ester Schaler Buchholz in *The Call of Solitude.* Otherwise we lose our authenticity. We say we "don't know who we are" anymore. We feel disconnected with ourselves and with the others that we refuse to get away from!

> **"I never found the companion**
> **that was so companionable as solitude."**
> —Henry David Thoreau

If we could look into the jaws of why we fear solitude, we'd find that it's not the jaws of a shark but more the gums of guppy.

Why are you uncomfortable or afraid to be alone? As a baby, your needs weren't met unless someone did something for you. You had to be near someone in order to survive. As you grew up, you may have associated being left alone with the inability to get what you want. It is no wonder then that the need to connect takes precedence over desire for aloneness.

15 Reasons you don't seize the solitude you need:
- You think it's selfish.
- You think it's frivolous and an expensive luxury.
- It's pioneering at this point and you're not comfortable being a pioneer. "(We're) not accustomed to the joys of solitude." —Edith Wharton

- You suspect that the truth of your life will show itself and you might not be able to handle it.
- It is difficult to admit that you want it.
- You're embarrassed to give "passionate attention to your life." —Virginia Wolf
- You don't know what to do with the time you spend alone.
- You're afraid you'll like it and want more of it.
- You've been "warned about solitary vices." —Jessamyn West
- You equate solitary time with quarantine.
- You have to work up the energy to ask for it and defend it.
- You risk offending someone by asking for it.
- You assume that you'll be labeled anti-social or eccentric.

**"To deliberately practice the art of solitude is
a difficult lesson to learn. And yet, once it is done,
(it) is incredibly precious."**
—Anne Morrow Lindbergh

Then why do it? Why bother risking all this in the pursuit of alone time? What do you get with solitude? What's the pay off?

- You can think and play with possibilities.
- Research shows that you solve problems better alone than with a spouse.
- You will experience an improvement in quality of life.
- When you do engage others, the experience will be richer.
- Solitude is necessary to develop creativity.
- Solitude is required to work the Inner Theatre Method— even 21 seconds of solitude has given you insights you didn't have before.

**"There are voices which we hear in solitude,
but they grow faint as we enter into the world."**
—Ralph Waldo Emerson

GET THESE VOICES BACK!

- Poor attachments, Type A personality, sleep deprivation and depression are all exacerbated by lack of alone time.
- Solitude affords a return to inner ease, a renewed sense of what we truly want thereby eliminating the need for sabotage...including the weight sabotage, the career sabotage and the financial sabotage.
- Solitude "feeds the soul." —Anne Morrow Lindbergh
- When you're alone, reducing stimulation decreases negativity and increases alertness helping to restore your ability to think clearly, be creative and maintain emotional calm.
- In religious terminology "solitude" meant the experience of oneness with one's God.

"The never-refreshed are really not that much fun to be around."
—Sarah Ban Breathnach in *Simple Abundance*

The fact that a basic requirement for life is not readily apparent is *not* unusual, Ester Schaler Buchholz points out. "Take thirst. Most often we get enough to drink through normal ingestion. Therefore, we are not automatically attuned to deprivation. But even people in the state of dehydration do not necessarily feel thirsty. So it is with the need for alonetime. In the past, the need for alonetime had been more or less satisfied in the natural course. Few today recognize this profound loss. Alonetime meets with social question, if not censure. People associate going it alone with unnecessary risk and being anti-social. We are grateful for 'time off' to engage in our own pursuits—like prisoners who are granted parole."

In Shel Silverstein's illustrated book *The Missing Piece,* a rolling circle searches the world for its "missing" piece, a slice-of-pie shaped wedge where its mouth is. It finally finds its missing piece, a wedge that fits. Now that the circle is "complete" it rolls faster, so fast that it can't take life in. With the wedge stuck in its mouth, the circle can't sing either. This story perfectly illustrates the problem of finding our "better half."

**"One thing worse than being alone—
wishing you were."**
—Bob Steele

There are more ways and more reasons to sabotage a romantic relationship than there are courts in this country. Some people just love the drama of it, comparing it to the rhythmic crashing of waves on a rocky shoreline. Some people are in denial that they actually dislike the opposite sex and are bent on destroying them one at a time. Other people are convinced that they are unlovable and when someone comes along who tries to love them, they have to prove them wrong. The complexity of the Coupling Sabotage is more evident because there are *two sets* of internal directors to consider.

If you suspect that you might have the desire to sabotage a relationship (especially when you review your past history), you can use the Inner Theatre method to discover what this sabotage is doing for you.

I have chosen to zero in on the plight of the Solitaire because it is so frequently overlooked. I used to think that natural Solitaires made up less than 10 percent of the population but recent research and my own observation says that that figure should be closer to 30 percent. And those people who mated and are happy about *living with another person* still require Alone time. Remember that your partner or your spouse may leave or die but your Internal Directors will always be with you. It's important that you give yourself the gift of solitude and stay in touch with them.

Chapter 12
Attitude And the
So What? Solution

"I just put three dollars in the change machine
and I'm still me."
—Jay Trachman

When I was ten years old, there a performance item on my report card. I didn't like it then and I still don't like it. If it were up to me, I'd make it *illegal* for this item to ever appear on any employee's Performance Appraisal! The item is: attitude.

I believe that you are entitled to your attitude. And I know that I don't always have a good one. Fortunately, it is not required.

What is attitude anyway?

Attitude is a combination of your MOOD and your PERSPECTIVE. Your mood is how you're feeling today. Your perspective is how you see the world. You and I are entitled to those things.

But attitude is attitude and behavior is behavior. They are not the same! Your behavior is what I can see and hear you doing. If anyone says that you have a bad attitude they are saying that because of what they have seen or heard.

Change tires,
change time zones,
change partners,
change planes,
change channels,
change your mind,
change the sheets,
change your name
but how do you CHANGE YOUR ATTITUDE?

If you ask someone to "change their attitude," what are they supposed to change?

Imagine that you work for a company and that you are the manager of the telephone receptionists. You have one receptionist that answers the phone in a voice reserved for fish markets, with the question, "Acme Company, what the *@#&! do you want?"

As the manager, you can tell this employee to "change their attitude" and what will likely happen? You'll get a defensive reaction. Or you can give the receptionist instruction like this: "I want you to change two things about the way you answer the phone. I want you to change the actual words you use. I want you to say, 'Acme Company, may I help you?' The second thing I want you to change is your tone of voice. I want something a little lighter, a little warmer. So change two things—the words and the way you say them. OK, got it?"

You have just given this person direction as if you were a stage director directing an actor. The receptionist knows specifically what changes to make and you have taken your hands off their attitude! You want this person to *play the part of a pleasant receptionist.*

It's none of your business if your employees, or your mate or your children have lousy attitudes. They are entitled to their lousy attitudes if they want them. And so are you.

"It simply isn't reasonable to expect yourself to feel good all the time."
—Barbara Sher

A professor at a Midwestern university once explained: "I worked for a college for a few years and I didn't like my schedule, I didn't like the dean and eventually I didn't like the college. I had a rotten attitude. But I did good work while I was there. My students didn't need to know that I had a bad attitude. I just didn't bring rotten behavior with me."

If you have a great attitude, that's *wonderful.* You'll have more fun and things will probably be easier for you. But when there's plant closures, layoffs, downsizing, traffic jams, office politics and a staff that can't agree on how to hang toilet paper, that's when you need my information. Some of us try living through these times expecting ourselves to somehow develop a good attitude. Nothing would get done if we had to wait for the right attitude.

It's OK for you to have a lousy attitude and it's OK for me to have a lousy attitude. I have told everyone who has ever worked for me that they are entitled to have a bad attitude. What isn't OK is lousy behavior—behavior that lacks courtesy, cooperation and creativity.

Attitude is not behavior. Attitude is attitude. Behavior is behavior. The magic, of course, is that if you change your behavior (and act courteously, cooperatively and creatively), you'll find your attitude improving on its own.

Employees have lives outside of the work place. Some of them are going through divorces, they have kids with drug problems, they have aging parents who need care, they may have financial problems. But when you create a work environment where everyone is expected to have great behavior *no matter what,* this happens: employees find coming to work is a refuge. Once they get themselves in gear by ten o'clock in the morning they have a good attitude.

Attitude is like a puppy that will follow along behind you...once *you* get moving!

I don't have a great attitude about food and weight. Anyone who has ever wanted to lose a few pounds knows that I don't wake up in the morning and say, "Wow! I get to deal with the appetite of a Green Bay Packer again today and all that food stuff! Lucky me!" No, 365 days a year, no time off for good behavior, no vacation from it, it is every day of my life! Do I like it? No. Am I successful at keeping the weight off? Yes! I don't have to have a great attitude about it—*thank heavens!* I just have to accept it and deal with it. If it were up to me ice cream would be a vegetable. But it isn't. And there is no food plan anywhere, no miracle cure that will let Alyce eat what she wants in the quantity that she wants and still be the size she wants. Trust me on this one.

If attitude determined altitude, I'd be under water.

Tell people who work for you that they are entitled to bad attitudes. They will stare at you like collies being taught chess. Explain *specifically* what kinds of behaviors you require in your work place. Period. Explain what acting courteously, cooperatively and creatively looks like and sounds like. (As a manager I did this myself so I know that it's possible.) Then explain that at any point in time when they feel that they *cannot* act courteously, cooperatively and creatively, there is a solution.

There is a piece of paper that comes around usually every other week and employees sign their names to that paper. When they sign their names that means that they agree to work courteously, cooperatively and creatively. So when they feel that they can no longer do that all they have to do is to NOT sign the paper. The paper is their paycheck.

Every time you sign your name to your paycheck you agree to play by the company's rules. If you agree to the rules, then whose rules are they? They're *your rules*.

It's easier to act yourself into a new way of thinking than to think yourself into a new way of acting.

When you pay $60 or $80 or $200 or $300 for a ticket to see some Big Name performer and you pay the parking structure just to park your car to see this event…and you show up on time and wait patiently in your seat…you don't care if Merle Haggard or Barbara Streisand is having a bad day and a matching bad attitude. You expect them to get up on that stage on time and to give it all they've got. You expect a great performance no matter what hell they may be living through at the moment.

Why should we expect anything less from a rental car agent, a check out clerk or a government employee? We're all being paid to get out there on the employment stage and perform.

Whether you're a bank vice-president or a nurse or a dry cleaning clerk, you are entitled to a bad attitude. What you're NOT entitled to is bad behavior.

On a *60 Minutes* interview Katherine Hepburn said, "I don't approve of my attitude."

**"Trying to force a positive attitude
is the surest way *not* to get something done."**
—Barbara Sher

So the next time you feel like you want to ask someone to "change their attitude," concentrate on the specific behaviors that you want changed instead. Ask yourself, "What gives me the impression that this person has a bad attitude? What are they doing, specifically, that makes me think this?" It will be something you can see or hear. Check list might include: tone of voice, stony silence, body language, procrastination, commitments broken, lack of action.

The next time someone asks you to "change your attitude," ask for more specific information. If you don't ask, you may change the wrong behavior.

It's easier to talk about behaviors than it is to talk about attitudes.

But isn't it a lie to act one way when you feel another way? Well, welcome to Planet Earth! It's easier and it's faster to change your behavior and *act as if.* Then *feel* your attitude change.

**"I couldn't wait for success
so I went ahead without it."**
—Jonathan Winters

I was hired to teach my communication course for a group of hospital employees. When I arrived at the teaching facility I noticed more than the usual amount of Personnel Department staff. They explained to me that only the afternoon before there had been a big lay off. Even employees who were very close to retiring were let go. "So people are going to be bleeding emotionally," they added. I asked if they were sure they wanted to go ahead with the training. They explained that they had been meeting at 2 A.M. that morning discussing just that question. And yes, they had decided to go on with things "as usual."

My communication course is a lively and interactive session so I was hoping it might even take the employees' minds off their employment situation. Now they were faced with much more work to do and far fewer people to handle it. Because I teach communication from a behavior stand point, I put in the part about attitude. Well, when I got to this part there was a noticeable shift in the room. I noticed shoulders dropping and tension lines eased in faces. "What I like about your program," one nurse said, "is your attitude about attitude. I don't have a good attitude about the hospital right now. I feel so much better now that I can have my bad attitude. It will make having the good behavior so much easier. And, you know, my patients don't need to know I have a bad attitude."

Now that's a real pro. Anyone who can get up on their stage and sing their song when their heart lies beating on the floor, that puts them in the pro category.

Fortunately you don't have to have a good attitude. I'm relieved by that because if a good attitude had been required to get the weight off, I'd still outweigh Jesse Ventura. If I had to have a good attitude to get my taxes paid on time or write a novel or deliver a speech on the same stage as Henry Kissinger, I wouldn't have been able to do any of those things either. I can be frustrated, afraid or intimidated and all these things just mean that I'm human. So give yourself a pat on the back for being human and now get on with it.

"Act as though it is impossible to fail."
—Dorothy Parker

Now I'm going to describe four scenes from a typical life. These are all real life situations people have described to me.

"I got a deal made on a house, got the kids enrolled in a new school and the deal didn't go through. My wife's going to be so upset..."

So what? Now what?

"I've eaten right, taken all the pills the doctor gave me and yet my blood sugar has been over 285 for two weeks. I did everything they said to do..."

So what? Now what?

"My uncooperative teenaged son with the black clothes, colored hair and combat boots—his principal just called, said he hasn't been in school for three days. This is the same son I wanted to see graduate from West Point…"

So what? Now what?

"I've got a loser on my team at work. I've tried everything to make it possible for him to succeed. He takes advantage of everybody. And everybody thinks I'm a good guy boss—I like it that everybody thinks I'm a nice guy…"

So what? Now what?

We need to stop kidding ourselves about the house—*find another one;* about the blood sugar—*you're diabetic, go take care of it;* about West Point—*you are not your children;* about the loser at work—*is this person ever going to improve their performance?* (Remember something happens when you stop lying to yourself: success.)

When you say "So what? Now what?" to yourself it allows three important things to happen:

1. You can now take the situation in as *information.*
2. You can now create a *strategy.*
3. You can now *act.*

There's a wonderful little story about a man who had a successful business for 30 years on the same corner. He was a barber and owned a small barber shop. He had put two kids through college; his daughter was in high school. Everything seemed to be going along well when right across the street developers put in one of those strip malls with a hair cutting franchise that posted a huge sign in the window: $6 HAIR CUTS. When the barber saw the sign he ran into his business and started penciling figures. He concluded that he couldn't even pay his rent if he charged only $6 for a hair cut. He would lose his business and his daughter would not be able to go to college.

Distraught the man went to see the rabbi and he said, "I've been on this corner for 30 years, I've always paid my bills and had a good business. I won't have money for college tuition. My daughter…" The rabbi, in his infinite wisdom, looked at the man and said, "So what? Now what?"

Stunned, the man went back to his barber shop. He looked at the big sign across the street and he looked around his little business. Finally he found a wooden sandwich board, one of those double-sided signs about 3 feet by 4 feet and he put the sign out on the sidewalk in front of his shop. In large letters he wrote: WE FIX $6 HAIRCUTS.

"So what? Now what?" puts things in perspective like nothing else. When all about you is chaos and wheel spinning, you can empower yourself by saying, "So what? Now what?" When you are so scared you're sure everyone is going to see your knees knocking, say, "So what? Now what?" When you want to buy something wonderful and you just found out you need to buy new tires instead, that's a big "So what? Now what?" You know what you need to do.

Chapter 13
The Concept of Land Mines

"Who knows how to make love stay?"
—Tom Robbins

You are surrounded by a mine field whether you know it or not. You created it, now let's look at it.

Your mine field consists of things that infuriate you. You may call these your "hot buttons" because when someone lands on them, you get hot. Your land mines may include things like broken promises, clogged salt shakers, the Department of Motor Vehicles, computer manuals or unreturned phone calls. For most people these are just irritants but for some people these are major land mines.

There are two things to remember about land mines:
1. They are unique to you. Our marvelous eccentric natures are never more obvious than when we're angry. What "gets your goat" doesn't even interest someone else's goat.
2. You need to *own* these land mines. Do not assume that other people can guess where your land mines are.

When you grasp the Concept of Land Mines, your life gets easier. It also allows you to do some interesting work with people in your life who are self-sabotaging.

You may be a fairly mild-mannered person which means that you are surrounded by a sparsely populated mine field. There's not much out there that would really make you mad. But when Tom Brockaw does a segment on the "Fleecing of America," you go ballistic. If the military buys one more $500 hammer you swear you're going to go nuts. When you hear one of these news stories you can do a non-stop 15-minute monologue that includes your "hard earned money," your last year's tax bill, the deficit, tax reform, campaign financing and then work in minimum wage, "cradle-to-grave security," and national parks. If no one interrupts you, your tirade can blossom into what you earned as a kid delivering newspapers, the demise of income averaging and end up e-mailing a nasty message to your senator. That's OK. At least now we know where one of your Land Mines is located. Your spousal unit may note this and make you a distracting dinner during Tom's next broadcast.

You don't really know yourself if you don't know where your Land Mines are. Unfortunately the way we discover them is when someone lands on one of them. You didn't know you could get so angry until you get a parking ticket and you know that you put enough money in the meter.

Land Mine Law #1 for the Rational Person: It is unfair to blow up at someone when they land on one of your land mines for the first time. Exceptions to this rule include anything that threatens your physical safety. Self-defense courses actually have to teach people to react harshly in potentially dangerous situations. Another exception would be flagrant acts of stupidity that threaten your property or security—the overnight guest who brings illegal drugs into your home, for instance. You have carte blanche to let your anger be known in obvious situations like these.

Land Mine Law #2 for the Rational Person: Locate your Land Mines and understand *what* they are even if you don't understand *why* they're there. Understanding the "why" is not required. Accept your quirks.

Example:

For some unknown reason you have an aversion to seeing apple cores in drinking glasses. You did not know that this was a Land Mine for you because you've never actually seen such a sight. Then one day your spouse or roommate is reading a book in your mutual living room and they enjoy an apple and a glass of milk. Several hours later as you pass through this room you notice that they've gone on to another activity and they have left behind this drinking glass and in the glass is the remainder of the eaten apple. This strikes you as a disgusting sight. Your blood pressure leaps several points. Your molars come together.

At this point you can say to yourself, I am having an irrational anger response here and this is really no big deal. If this is your response, you have chosen the slow route to insanity via repression and passive aggression. You will get back at your spouse or roommate later today and they won't know why. You probably won't know either. You will leave the cap off of their favorite pen, take the last piece of pizza or leave the headlights on in their car.

Or you can pick up the glass and yell at the "offending" partner about what a disgusting slob they are. This is an option. Some couples communicate beautifully this way. Your partner may yell back that you're nuts and you can come back with yes, but "you knew that when you married me" and they may kiss you and say that was the best day of their life. This whole scene is possible but not likely.

But what if you did this...

You take the milky glass with the apple core in it to your partner and you say, "This is going to sound sort of weird but you know, I seem to have an aversion to apple cores in drinking glasses. I didn't even know I had this Land Mine but I gotta tell ya, this is a Land Mine with me. Do us both a favor and when you've got an apple core, don't put it in a drinking glass, OK?"

Land Mine Law #3 for the Rational Person: If they have been so notified, people are allowed three hits on one of your Land Mines before you're allowed to blow. Why three?

The first offense was probably done out of complete ignorance of your unusual Land Mine. The second one is slipsies—oops! forgot! The third offense, however, is a message.

It may take years of living together to locate many of your Land Mines and it's OK if they are unusual, you just have to take responsibility for them. Be as eccentric as you want, just communicate so that your mate stands a chance of being successful with you. If you and your partner have agreed to the Concept of Land Mines and you have clearly explained about the drinking glass and the apple core, you have now owned your part of it.

Imagine your partner leaves the third milk glass in the

living room and there is clearly an apple core in it. This is no longer just an apple core in a drinking glass. It is now a message. It is tempting to say that the message is "bad" but maybe not. If you are living with someone who doesn't want your relationship, wouldn't you want to know that?

If you're really rational—like *saintly* rational—you might go to your partner with the drinking glass in your hand and repeat your request that you hope you never again in your whole life will see such a sight. Then ask if there is some obnoxious behavior of *yours* that you could *trade* for never seeing another apple core in a drinking glass. Your partner may respond with something like, "Yeah, you throw the newspaper out before I get a chance to read it!" OK, now you can agree to not throw the newspaper away in exchange for the apple core in the drinking glass. This is called behavior negotiation. It works with spouses, teenagers, roommates, parents and employees.

I once traded "advance notice that you need money for school" for "singing in the shower." The last minute "I-need-$20" request from my teenager usually came the day *after* I had done my banking. A couple of requests for more planning and greater lead time didn't work so I suggested a behavioral trade. She requested "no singing in the shower." I didn't even know I *sang* in the shower! Both requests were honored and peace prevailed.

What happens if the request still isn't honored? Let's say you have complied with your partner's request and even taken out two subscriptions to the daily newspaper and you never even touch your partner's newspaper. What if you still find apple cores in drinking glasses in the living room? You've been a good camper and honored your half of the agreement. The odd occurrence of the purposeful behavior of the apple core should give you pause for thought.

Aggressive behavior would be: "George, if I find one more apple core in one more drinking glass, I'm going to spray paint your lucky game shirt."

Passive aggressive behavior would be: Lacing all of his apples with a powerful liquid laxative.

What would you do? What is the message of the apple

core?

Land Mine Law #4 for the Rational Person: Know that other people have Land Mines and that you may inadvertently land on one. If an explosion occurs, explain the Concept of Land Mines and that, had you known that Land Mine was there, you would have respected it. Now that you know, you promise to avoid it in the future because your relationship with this person is important to you. Unless, of course, it *isn't*.

Land Mine Law #5 for the Rational Person: Do not bother to attempt to talk someone out of their Land Mines! This is a fruitless waste of time and it's insulting. Better to say, "Wow! That's a goofy Land Mine but OK, I've got it. I can work with that."

One couple had a simple technique that would make good advice for any partnership. They shared a blank journal. They lived together but they also recognized the importance of written communication. Writing notes to someone you live with is a very attractive thing to do. Their system with the journal went like this: Complete two sentences...

"I really like it when _____."
"I really don't like it when _____."

They honored the idea that neither one of them were mind readers and their goal was that they train each other to stay in love. The rule was, you have 48 hours to fill in the blanks and hand the book to the other person. They have 48 hours to complete the same two sentences and hand it back. Entries into the journal included things like:

"I really like it when you replace the toilet paper."

"I really don't like it when you leave your shoes on the staircase."

"I really like it when you scratch my back."

"I really don't like it when you're away."

Still Life With Woodpecker is a novel by Tom Robbins and in it he addresses the problem of staying in love. Most of us would agree with Robbins that the challenge in relationships is not falling in love but rather not falling out of love.

We assume that "if you loved me, you'd know what I want" and this is grossly unfair. What you want is not obvious. There's a certain amount of training that is required for all lasting relationships and that goes for manager/employee, parent/offspring, partner/house mate and purchaser/supplier.

A manager who wonders if they have a sabotaging employee can go to this person and say, "You can do anything you want in our work place but the one thing you must never do is to push this purple button here on the wall. That's the only requirement for a long and happy employment with us." Then see how long it takes them to hit that button. I'm speaking symbolically here but you get the concept. Be very clear about what behaviors you need—what employees will be rewarded for and what they can be penalized for—and then watch what happens.

Land Mine Law #6 for the Rational Person: Respect the small things.

"There's a tendency today to absolve individuals of moral responsibility and treat them as victims. <u>What limits people is lack of character</u>. What limits people is that they don't have the imagination to star in their own movie, let alone direct it."
—Tom Robbins

Chapter 14
How To Avoid Hiring
a Sabotaging Employee

You've been promoted to supervisor or manager. You've never hired anybody in your life. And you're instantly expected to do it well and do it NOW.

Hiring people is not just a line item on your job description. You will be judged on how well you do this. Upper management will be looking at your staff turnover, *especially the staff you've hired.*

Hiring is a critical activity and your success as a manager depends on how well you can find, interview and *select* each person who works for you. All of a sudden hiring becomes not this annoying thing you have to shoehorn into your already hectic life—if you're a savvy manager you will realize that it is as critical as electricity in the emergency room of a hospital. Without it, you're dead meat.

I have never had to fire anybody I've hired.

Part of that has been luck and part of that has been because of the following advice you're going to read now. I hope you're reading this *before* you hire anyone so that you too will be able to say: "I've never had to fire anybody I've hired." If you already have, then may be you will be able to say: "I've never had to fire anybody I've hired *since I read Alyce's advice.*"

Given the fact that roughly 50% of all Americans have sabotaged a job at least once in their lives, how can you, the savvy management person, avoid hiring the sabotaging employee?

1. Recognize how serious the function of hiring is and devote your attention to it. Don't leave it up to personnel or any staff person regardless of how busy you are. If you're a control freak you don't need to be told this.

2. Understand that employee sabotage comes in four flavors—get your management antennae sensitive to discovering it. The motivations behind the sabotaging employee can be as varied as: they're grouchy and they just don't want anybody to succeed, all the way up to they'd secretly like to start their own business and don't even know it themselves. They're waiting to get fired so they'll have an excuse. As a manager, you don't have time to discover the whys for the sabotage, you just need to find the potential saboteur and eliminate them from your list of candidates. If you select wrong enough of the time, upper management will be looking to eliminate you.

Employees sabotage: **time, stuff, space and information.** They sabotage the company goals, other people, the strategic plan, the team but HOW they do it comes out and down to: time, stuff, space and information.

Sabotaging Time looks like this: procrastination, deadlines not met, being late for anything, water cooler gab fests, long lunches, working late too often (this isn't the sign of worker devotion, it's a sign of a worker with a bad time management problem and a potential martyr), wasting everybody's time by running boring and unnecessary meetings, prolonged playing on the computer, not respecting other people's time.

Sabotaging Stuff looks like this: misuse of company funds (money is stuff), misfiling, consistent screw ups of audiovisual set ups, damaging equipment, wasting everything from paper to gasoline, "borrowing" some other employee's stuff without permission, losing stuff, "misplacing" stuff, shared tools and equipment left screwed up for the next person (jammed copy machines to D9 Caterpillars).

Sabotaging Space looks like this: occupying more area than is necessary, not comprehending that every square foot of space has a dollar value attached to it and then operating accordingly, invading other employee's space with their stuff or their bodies, rendering any space (locker rooms to lunch rooms) less desirable than when they entered, using a space for inappropriate activity.

Sabotaging Information looks like this: eliminating key players from a meeting, not returning phone calls, leaving e-mail or phone messages with a "just contact me" message instead of relaying requests, withholding critical information, "forgetting" to inform others so that they can be successful, "accidentally misinforming" others, inaccuracies on resume or job application, hiding information from clients/customers, lying to the press or fellow employees or *anybody*.

The President of the United States is a federal employee and every time we've come close to impeaching one of them, it's been because they have sabotaged all four of these elements. Employee sabotage is not exclusive to entry level positions.

Mini-Quiz

The City Manager of a good-sized American city made front page news when he was arrested for stealing a $9 pair of sunglasses. His salary was in the six figures. That made for interesting news. What made it fascinating news was that this *wasn't the first time he'd done it*. The city's law enforcement people had let the first offense go because of the guy's position.

OK, class, this is a true story. What do you deduce from the City Manager's behavior?

If you said, he's a nut and needs help, you're probably right but leave that for others' speculation. It's none of our business. What *is* our business, especially with government employees is: *this man is sabotaging his job*. His message is: "I don't want to be City Manager."

So you may ask, why didn't he just resign? He didn't resign because he *didn't know* he didn't want to be City Manager (or to use my language, he didn't know there was a part on the inside that didn't want to be City Manager anymore) and even if he *did* know it, he couldn't admit it (for whatever reasons). And, we can suspect, the element of public humiliation was something he actually wanted. Remember there is the awful phenomenon of human behavior that makes us recreate what we "knew" as children—and if you, like the City Manager, were consistently humiliated then you will come to expect and manage to bring into your life that same humiliation.

The City Manager got what he wanted: (a) relieved of his position and (b) publicly humiliated and (c) treatment and sympathy for his "problem" and (d) no chance of working and staying in that city.

How can you keep the City Manager and people like him *off your payroll?*

Don't hire them in the first place.

3. The hiring process begins with the resume and job application. So put a filter on your awareness when you read these documents and screen for behavioral sabotage.

How many jobs has this person had?

How many successful enterprises have they been part of?

Do they appear to have an uncanny knack for selecting loser outfits?

Have they selected their employment carefully in the past?

How have they presented themselves on the page? If you're hiring a payroll accountant, alarm bells should go off in your head when you see an application with handwriting you can't read, misuse of grammar and smeared ink. What qualities are you looking for in this employee...and are they reflected for you on paper? Don't ignore the signs. If you're hiring somebody to install sheetrock, you may not care about misspelled words...maybe.

What *high school* activities did they participate in? Achievers get started early. Knowing their outside activities will also give you a window into the kinds of ambitions this person really has. If this person was an active member of Future Teachers of America, for instance, are you hiring them for a position where they will sit alone in a room without human contact for days at a time? Conversely, if this person won blue ribbons with the Future Farmers of America and you're hiring forest rangers, that might be a great big plus. Do you need an employee who has a devoted respect for deadlines? Were they on the school newspaper or yearbook staff? *Great!*

Successful career counselors take people back to their childhoods in an effort to connect real passion to real jobs. When people are doing what they *want* to do, they're usually good at it. The high school treasurer of the chess club may make an unlikely candidate for the position of glad-handing Welcome Wagon host.

If your candidate spent their high school years under the oil pan of an old street rod and you're hiring bus mechanics, you may have a match there.

As a manager, you need to remember that you cannot be all things to all people. Your task as Hiring Guru is to fit round pegs into round holes, even when square pegs are presenting themselves as round pegs.

4. The interview: your butt is on the line, not theirs. Be rested, be prepared and don't do more than 4 interviews in one day. If this person will be working with both men and women, team interview with an opposite sex partner.

Interviewing Tips for Hiring

<u>Ask open ended questions</u>. Questions that can't be answered yes or no. Past performance is a great indicator of self-sabotage.

<u>Team interview, if possible</u>. Team interviewing allows you to take special note of how much time the candidate looks and responds to you and how much time to your partner. Do they seem to only want to look at the male in the room? Are they obviously more comfortable talking to the female? Do they speak only to the person who is in the "power position"? Or is it equal and comfortable communication coming from your candidate?

<u>Most important: Ask situation questions</u>.

What's that?

Situation questions are scenarios that you create from real life happenings in your office. There's no "right" and "wrong" to these questions; they are judgment calls about real life.

For instance, let's say you're hiring a mail room/errand person. You ask this question: "You have payroll checks and $30,000 worth of cash receivables. You are in the company van headed to the bank. The van breaks down on the freeway. The cell phone battery is dead. What do you do?"

You're hiring a staff printer and you ask: "You have 3 jobs all requiring two hours of press time. It is 2:00 P.M and they are all due at 5:00 P.M. What do you do?"

Receptionist candidate: "You've got the company president's mother on Line 1, an irate customer on Line 2 and *60 Minutes'* Mike Wallace has just phoned in on Line 3. What do you do?"

Manager candidate: "How do you fill positions and select new employees—what's your criteria or what's your system?"

<u>Ask team questions</u>: You can even create symbolic questions, such as—on a football team, what position would you want to play?—to get a feel for their comfort level in team situations. If you don't need a team player, then don't hire for one. But when will that be? Until there is a job description for "hermit", we're all somehow connected to a team.

<u>Follow EEO guidelines</u>: It's not a straight jacket; it's good business.

<u>Watch for phrases</u>:   "but what I really want to do is…"
"they wouldn't let me…"
"I couldn't get them to…"
"It wasn't my fault…"
"They had lousy equipment…"
"Sorry I was late…"

Watch body language. The problem with body language is that people take an isolated body gesture and conjure up all sorts of conclusions. Crossed arms means they're closed—well, not necessarily, it's a comfortable thing to do. If, however, you're getting a lot of interesting body language (hand over the mouth constantly may indicate there's more they really want to say, scratching nose is a gesture of an untruth according to recent research, repeated shrugging indicative of not owning responsibility) should cause your self-sabotage antennae to twitch.

Look for any incongruencies. Has their behavior matched what they are saying? Do they say "left" and go "right"? "My goal in life is to help all the children of the world. I took my college graduation money and went on a cruise to Hawaii." or this: "I really want to pay off my college loans," and then 40 seconds later, "I bought myself this really great new SUV!"

Don't fill in the silences. An American is uncomfortable with 3 seconds of silence in a conversation and extremely uncomfortable with 10 seconds. Let your candidate fill the silences and frequently they will give you information you need to make a hiring decision.

Don't ask stupid questions. What is a stupid question? My favorite is: what do you want to be doing in 5 years? I think the response to this question that I liked the most is: (speaking to the interviewer) "I want your job."

Trust your instincts. Cops tell us that victims almost always have a creepy sense of apprehension just before a crime happens. They tell us all to trust that instinct and act on it *even if it goes against rational thinking*. The same advice goes for hiring. Just as the interview is ending, ask yourself this question: "Is this person going to sabotage their job?" Then listen hard to your internal decision maker.

I most sincerely hope that you will be able to say: "I've never had to fire anybody I've hired," because it's expensive, it's painful for everybody, it's a major stressor. A person being fired experiences a 200% jump in their stress level but the person *doing the firing experiences a 500% increase* in their stress levels.

Hire well. Sleep well.

Chapter 15
Your Evil Twin/Your Warrior

**"I have these parts—optimist and pessimist,
depressed and exultant—all accessible to me
and my work."**
—Richard Avedon

So how are you supposed to lose weight when you've got a more powerful part of You that wants the weight on? How can you get your novel written when your Internal Writer can't be heard? How can you have a successful relationship when part of you atrophies without solitude?

"We have met the enemy and he is us."
—Pogo (Walt Kelly)

It's no wonder people speak of their "inner demons" and are mystified by their own behavior. "The devil made me do it." Psychotherapists write about the Inner Saboteur. One book on the current best seller list says that when you are derailed by fear or feel sorry for yourself that this is your authentic self's evil twin: the ego. It is as if there is this awful part of us that takes over when we open the refrigerator or go shopping.

There is no "evil twin." It's all You. And even though I have an inner character who believes that having extra weight on (100 pounds!) will somehow protect me, I remain a normal weight. That's because I don't think any parts are evil. Just the opposite. These are Survival Mechanisms and they love you and want to take care of you. They just have some goofy wiring, that's all.

Your parts, your internal voices, love you more than anyone on the outside of You ever has. Their *expression* of that love is to protect you from having money, having health, having a successful career or relationship. They are cunning, baffling, powerful and effective. But it's a full time job and they may be exhausted from working so very hard. They've been doing all this work for You and the thanks they get is being labeled your "evil twin."

You need to *take care of these parts* of You as well as they have taken care of you. When you stop your ceaseless activity and get quiet and listen, they will talk to you. You will find out what they've been doing for you and why. Once you know that your benefit is protection or connection to others or rebellion or moving back to Seattle, then be smart enough to give yourself that benefit. Honor your voices, decode their loving messages and love them enough to give them what they want.

There is no "enemy" within. If there is any enemy at all it is the non-stop fax-paced world that keeps you separated from your Inner Selves. With a to-do list in one hand and a cell phone in another, you move through your day listening to everybody but the people who count, those people inside your head. We get e-mail and v-mail and snail mail. We really need to pay attention to i-mail (inner mail)—those messages from your *intra*net.

The next time one of your friends whines about losing weight *while they are eating a hot fudge sundae,* just know that they aren't checking their i-mail. The circuits are lit up but nobody's answering.

Instead of trying to "outsmart the enemy within" why not give them what they want? Lots of it. Then sabotage isn't necessary! One popular book today suggests that you tell your ego to shut up, then turn on some beautiful music and drown it out. Hey, I'm tellin' you that even "Louie, Louie" played at mega-decibel level will not outshout my inner team. I bow to their power and I'd rather have them as friends—misguided sometimes, quirky certainly—than feel that I have enemies within.

YOU ARE THE GUARDIAN
OF YOUR "CHILDREN."

I went to the South Pacific to take an intensive course that involved history, culture and ancient Polynesian religion. During a demonstration about a tradition, some of us were selected to be "guardians" for other members of the class. Those we were guarding were to reexperience a trauma from their pasts. At an appropriate moment they could ask for help from their "guardians" and we were to defend and attack the nemesis from the past. We guardians were "armed" with long sticks the size of shepherd's staffs.

Words on a page are not adequate to tell you what kind of energy soared through me when my charge, in full anguish, asked for my help. He was not just *remembering,* he was *reliving* a situation with a cruel relative. I lit into "her" with a strength that I did not know that I possessed. My sense of protection for this fellow student surprised me and certainly him. I was Mother Tiger defending her cub as if more than both our lives depended on it.

You can only *experience this sensation,* you can't learn about it from anyone telling you about it. It was a truly amazing demonstration. I learned that it was an honor to serve as the guardian, it was not an obligation. I learned that because I *accepted the responsibility* to defend and protect, when it was time, I felt it with full fury. I learned that when *asked* I would respond with such intensity that there would be no room for question. I learned that I have a Warrior within that can be counted on to respond with swift and fiery energy to care for others.

I didn't know this student's name but I felt that a part of me would protect him for the rest of his life. There is no measurement to explain the intensity demonstrated by this ancient tradition.

Long ago it was part of human life to defend and protect our families, our villages, our communities. The closest we come today is defending the honor of Green Bay at a pro football game. We have lost touch with our inner warriors because that intense fierceness is not appropriate in our modern day world. Or is it?

If I could be a good guardian for this fellow student, then couldn't I also be a good guardian for someone else? Did I ever need a guardian for my Self? Aren't there times when an inner part of me has needs and could use a champion? Isn't it possible that this inner warrior could be the guardian of all those parts of me that need it?

Aren't there times—buffet lines and social events—when only warrior energy will keep you away from the dessert table? Doesn't it take warrior energy to finish writing a book when it's really a perfectly beautiful autumn day outside? Isn't *fierceness required* when you've got an idea for a new business and only you can make it happen? Wouldn't a warrior know what to do when you come to a big So What? Now What?

If I had demonstrated that I could be a trusted warrior for someone else, then I could also do it for mySelf. Two things would be required, just as before. In order to be the guardian, I would:

1. *accept the responsibility.*
2. be there when *asked.*

I could no longer pretend that I did not have a fierceness capable of active protection. If I could do this for myself, I would feel wrapped in security. I would know that I am fully protected and guarded by someone I could trust. What a marvelous thing!

If you can't seem to get things done, your warrior is asleep. If you are in an abusive relationship, your inner guardian has abandoned you. If you've started college and then wandered away, you lack your warrior.

Your inner warrior can look after the Fat Person on the inside of you that wants the weight on. The warrior can champion their cause—protection, connectedness, security. Sometimes only warrior energy can make it happen.

If you were given the responsibility for watching over a friend's prize-winning dog, would you accept the responsibility? Could you be counted on to care for this expensive animal? Or would you feed it garbage, inject it with alcohol and tobacco products and expose it to unhealthy environments? If you wouldn't care for a dog that way, then why do you do this to yourself?

The ancient Polynesians declaration (prayer): "I am the guardian, I am the warrior, I am the keeper of my children" means being the guardian of our own empires—that kingdom between our ears—and the "children" are the parts of ourselves that need our care.

There is no "enemy within" only children who need a guardian.

Many of you reading this have had situations in your life....you've had bad things happen...I wish bad things hadn't happened to you.

As children you did not get all the recognition you deserved. I'd like to give recognition to every creative kid who heard: "Who do you think you are?"

For every fat or odd looking kid who got teased or abused, I am so very sorry that that happened to you. I wish all children could be raised in happy homes, secure and not harassed.

For every kid whose parents weren't there—they failed you; it wasn't your fault, I wish you had not been betrayed.

For every kid who raised themselves, I wish you had been loved more and honored more.

I applaud you, I recognize your efforts—I wish I could have been there for you.

I wish you could have been there for me. I know you would have done a good job.

What's Your Sabotage? 237

Programs
(taught by Alyce Cornyn-Selby)

SELF-SABOTAGE & CREATIVE PROCRASTINATION

**"Self-sabotage is when we say we want something —
then go about making sure it doesn't happen."**
Wouldn't it be *great* if you could talk to yourself and *really
mean it?* New Year's resolutions, writer's block, sales goals,
weight loss — apply the master's technique for overcoming
self-defeating behavior. Recognize sabotage in others. From
America's **High Priestess of Procrastination** and author of
the *Procrastinator's Success Kit.*

WINNING: WHY WINNERS WIN

What winners have and what they *don't have;* the Unruly Role
of Attitude in winning; The First Rule of Holes and the
Unwritten American Constitution. From the author of *Why
Winners Win.* Great keynote!

TEAMWORK & TEAM SABOTAGE

What makes Americans uniquely qualified to sabotage teams?
8 Keys to the environment that makes team*work;* the One
Sure Killer of teams; 28 ways to encourage teamwork. From
the author of *Teamwork & Team Sabotage.*

COMMUNICATION & COOPERATION

Overcome "change resistance" and get cooperation through
effective and *efficient* communication; the backward effect of
Attitude; 6 Steps to Persuasion; the Essence of Self-
Confidence; getting behaviors you want from others.

ARE YOU FROM ANOTHER PLANET OR *WHAT*?

For those who work with, sell to or meet with both men and
women, this dynamite program of research *and solutions*
reaches the mysterious gender differences that affect communication. You'll say, "Oh, *that's* why that happens!"

HIRE THE AUTHOR
503-232-0433

How about some comedy ...

The War Bride is the comedy "journalist" who reports on the news from the War Front of American Life. Direct from the DMZ of cell phones, Day-Timers, the Battle of the Bulge and power struggles over the remote control, this reporter can shake up the troops with laughter. Census reports, today's newspapers and research conclusions about YOU!

Special requests:

Meeting Effectiveness: We've *Got* to
Stop Meeting Like This!
Performance Appraisals: Creating A System That Works
Making Your Mark: *That's Marketing!*
Change, Open Minds & Attitude
The Lost Art of Having Fun
"Good Grief, I Sound Just Like My Mother!"
Success Story: From Scheduled Downsizing to a National
Winning Team

"Alyce is the strongest solution you can get without a prescription."

Alyce Cornyn-Selby, highly acclaimed speaker and nationally recognized master on the subject of **sabotage** (overcoming self-defeating behaviors), instructs fighter pilots, nurses, bank presidents, FBI agents, corporations and associations from Honolulu to London.

She isn't a speech; she's an *event*.

Manager of the most award-winning communications team of its kind in the country, Alyce is uniquely qualified to illustrate *winning* in the world of work.

Award-winning scriptwriter and film producer, Alyce brings visual drama and comedy to her programs. With an early background of adversity and obesity **(she maintains a 100-pound weight loss),** Alyce also brings humor.

AUTHENTICITY: Alyce ties her personal story of being perpetually terrified and "unemployable" to becoming a successful corporate executive — and the simple and profound lessons learned on the way. "Management does *not* have to be a form of advanced adult day care."

Honored in *Who's Who* publications in the U.S. and abroad for her research on American attitudes and behaviors. Alyce has been called:
THE HIGH PRIESTESS OF PROCRASTINATION.
Alyce is the author of eight books including the ever popular *Procrastinator's Success Kit*—still being requested and reprinted after ten years!

ABC, CBS, USA Cable, NBC, *Reader's Digest, This Week, Psychology Today, Journal of Commerce* and *Successful Meetings* have all featured Alyce's innovative solutions.

A is for Attitude. She's got one. Clearly, Alyce knows something you may want to hear.

WHY WINNERS WIN

What traits do winners have?
Is the *self-confident* winner FACT or MYTH?
...And...can anyone be a winner?

Alyce Cornyn-Selby, whose ground-breaking
research on American attitudes and behaviors
has taken her across the U.S., now investigates
the often surprising world of the winner.

Why Winners Win is about:
- 6 things winners have
- 3 things they don't seem to have
- The Unwritten American Constitution
- People that winners avoid and why
- Failure 101: Jack's class
- The role of attitude in winning:

  How important is it anyway?
  What if I just don't feel like it today?
- The seductive power of a name
- The First Rule of Holes

Mega-Mini Book: Size 5 1/2 x 4 1/4

**Here is: How to keep winning when the rules keep changing;
being successful even when you don't feel like it..**

Alyce Cornyn-Selby--winner at weight loss, winner of awards for design,
photography and scriptwriting, winner at corporate communications,
and winning entrepreneur--researched winners in
business, sales, sports, government and education
for this uncommon, unconventional
and right-on-the-money look at winning.

**INTRIGUED? So was Microsoft, Bank of America, U.S. Forest Service and scores
of businesses and conferences who have heard this inspiring look at winning!**

TAPE AND BOOK ARE **NOT** IDENTICAL.

TAPE: (Audiocassette) Why Winners Win..$8.95
BOOK: Why Winners Win..$8.95

SELF SABOTAGE

"Self sabotage is when we say we want something and then go about making sure it doesn't happen."

Self sabotage. We've all done it. Self sabotage is when we act against our own best interests. We are *mysteries* to ourselves! We have no idea why we sabotage our careers, our finances, our exercise and weight programs.

Alyce says: "This can stop." Internationally recognized expert on behavior and achievement, Alyce Cornyn-Selby has researched the phenomenon of self sabotage for 15 years. She has created a system for overcoming self-defeating behaviors. "The system is *using you* every day of your life...now you can turn around and *use it!*"

Human behavior will finally make sense when you've heard: Alyce.

Every manager will eventually have to deal with an employee who is sabotaging their own job. You or someone you work with *or live with* is sabotaging something--either way, your life is being affected by it.

Alyce has taught this bank presid[...] pil[...] [...]ces [...]ss the U.S., [...]itain and Canada.

The system you will learn in this special videotaped program is for:
 walking away from procrastination,
 achieving sales and business goals,
 completing education, ending Writer's Block,
 weighing what you want to weigh and dropping financial sabotage.

Alyce Cornyn-Selby used her system to take off 100 pounds and keep it off. As a manager, she applied her system and created the most award-winning corporate communications team of its kind in the country. She knows something you want to hear.

VIDEOTAPE: Self Sabotage...**$29.**

This novel optioned to Warner Bros.--will it see the silver screen?

"Think of the American male as a teapot...
he will only pour out the truth when tipped over..."

The late Travis Duncan,
an unusual 37-year old woman,
bequeathes an estate worth over $23,000,000
to her ex-lovers. Her will stipulates that these men
must meet for one night and answer one question.
The man who answers the question correctly, wins.
The question is:
WHAT DO YOU ALL HAVE IN COMMON?

Seven men arrive in
Portland, Oregon to hear the terms of the will.
Five men stay to share their lives
in an effort to determine their commonality.
Each man is both despicable
and likable, depending on *your perspective*.

DID SHE LEAVE ME ANY MONEY?
is a rollicking ride that reinforces the
precious spirit of nonconformity.

The story depends on *your* perspective...
...on what *you* value.

DID SHE LEAVE ME ANY MONEY?

Alyce P. Cornyn-Selby

— Hmmm. This is interesting...

by
ALYCE CORNYN-SELBY

"A female Tom Robbins."
--*St. Martin's Press*

"Plot is unique, writing style is enticing."
--*Atlantic Monthly*

"The ending just right...make a fine film!"
--*Downtowner*

"A novel. A philosophical comedy."

BOOK: Did She Leave Me Any Money?..$11.95

TEAMWORK & TEAM SABOTAGE

Why do employees sabotage teams?

Teams produce results. You produce a team. Team building information is everywhere, but no where else can you find the solution to the inevitable TEAM SABOTAGE.

The author: "I was given 4 departments that were scheduled for downsizing--*but* we didn't get the axe--we became the most award-winning communications team of its kind in the country." Learn the keys from someone who knows.

Learn cultural quirks that make us uniquely qualified to sabotage teamwork. Essential for budget-cutting, up-against-the-wall, do-more-with-less, who's-got-time teams from a manager who has been there.

THE KEY:
8 environmental factors determine whether they'll act as a team. Do you know what they are?

Plus:
. solutions for productivity and cooperation *despite everything!*

. 28 ways to encourage Teamwork.

. The Scoreboard--why it's magic; why a team will die without it.

. attitude and "dark day" strategies.

A must for any serious team regardless of size or purpose.

One Fortune 500 company bought 7,000 copies of this book--every new employee gets a copy! Hewlett-Packard, Wacker, Tektronix, Boeing, U.S. West, police and fire departments buy this book in <u>quantity</u>!

"Nobody delivers Alyce Information and nobody delivers like Alyce. She changed my life."
--NCAA Coach of the Year, Bill Ballester

BOOK AND TAPE ARE IDENTICAL.
Mega-Mini Book: Size 5 1/2 x 4 1/4
TAPE: (Audiocassette) Team & Team Sabotage...$8.95
BOOK: Teamwork & Team Sabotage..$8.95

Internet Orders: **www.justalyce.com**
(different shipping rates apply)
Credit Card or Phone Orders: **1-800-937-7771**
(different shipping rates apply)

Alyce's books have been quoted in:
Reader's Digest, USA Today, Psychology Today, Successful Meetings
Writer's Digest, Daily Journal of Commerce, Competitive Advantage--
there's something here you need TODAY!

ORDER FORM

"*Learn* something! And become a more
interesting person!"

MAIL-IN ORDERS OVER $25--FREE SHIPPING!

QUANTITY	TITLE	TOTAL
$12.95	Procrastinator's Success Kit (Book)	
$8.95	Take Your Hands Off My Attitude! (Book)	
$11.95	Did She Leave Me Any Money? (Book)	
$29.00	VIDEO: Self Sabotage	
$8.95	Teamwork (Book)	
$8.95	Teamwork (Tape)	
$8.95	Alyce's FAT CHANCE (Book)	
$8.95	I Used To Be Fat (Tape)	
$8.95	Why Winners Win (Book)	
$8.95	Why Winners Win (Tape)	
$15.95	What's Your Sabotage? (Book)	
	TOTAL	

★ Shipping, $2 per item: _____

FREE SHIPPING!
For mail-in orders over $25!
On prepaid MAIL-IN Orders ONLY!

Checks payable: **BEYNCH PRESS**, 1928 S. E. Ladd Ave., Portland, OR 97214

Name: _____

Address: _____

City: _____ State: _____ Zip: _____

For Credit Card or Phone Orders: 1-800-937-7771
Note: Different shipping rates apply for phone orders...ask for details.